Commercial Lending
Basics

Commercial Lending Basics

Edward K. Gill

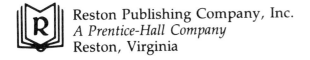
Reston Publishing Company, Inc.
A Prentice-Hall Company
Reston, Virginia

Library of Congress Catalog Card Number 82-83689
ISBN 0-8359-0881-X

PRINTED IN THE UNITED STATES OF AMERICA

Contents

Preface

Financing the needs of the business community is both complex and challenging. Financial service professionals entering this field for the first time can be overwhelmed by the intricacies of the commercial lending process.

Commercial Lending Basics is designed for all professionals who need a foundation on which to build commercial lending expertise. It introduces important terms and concepts. It examines the steps that must be taken before a commercial loan is granted. It reviews topics that range from financial statement analysis to policy formulation.

All lending activities carry a degree of risk. Commercial lending is no exception. This book was created to help individuals and organizations reduce that risk through a more complete understanding of the issues.

The author is grateful to others who have helped bring about this book. Special thanks go to John Deming, Ray Devery and George Leonard, Jr., who reviewed the manuscript. Their thoughtful comments are appreciated.

The author also extends a particular appreciation to The Institute of Financial Education which commissioned this text. At The Institute special thanks go to P. Gerald McEnany and Jean Lou Hess for their coordination and editorial support.

Dale C. Bottom
President
The Institute of Financial Education

Edward K. Gill
Boise State University

Commercial Lending
Basics

1

The Commercial Lending Environment

OBJECTIVES

After reading Chapter 1, you should be able to:

- Describe the economic significance of commercial lending;
- Cite five examples of interest rates and indicate whether each is administered or determined by free-market forces;
- Explain the concept of the yield curve and how it is used to interpret the structure of interest rates;
- Summarize at least three factors that influence interest rates;
- Define fiscal policy, monetary policy and money supply (M1);
- Compare financial institutions in terms of their major asset and liability categories;
- List at least five sources of commercial credit besides commercial banks.

The environment of commercial lending is determined by economic conditions and by those involved with making commercial loans. These influences are felt almost continuously by those people who work in commercial lending. The purpose of this chapter is to bring these environmental influences–particularly interest rate considerations–into focus before discussing more specific aspects of commercial lending.

ECONOMIC IMPORTANCE OF COMMERCIAL LENDING

Financial institutions that become involved with commercial lending enter a field of credit that is large and of great importance to the American economy. At the end of 1980, the total debt of U.S. corporations, not including financial intermediaries, was almost $1.2 trillion. Of this amount, almost two-thirds was in the form of debt securities (bonds and similar instruments) and mortgages. The remaining $400 billion of debt is in the form of commercial loans, the primary focus of this text (see Figure 1-1). This $400 billion only applies to corporations. If the total were known for all single proprietorships and partnerships in the U.S., the volume of commercial loans outstanding might well exceed $1 trillion.

Commercial lending is important to our economy. Business loans provide the funds for new businesses and for the renewal and expansion of existing businesses. Few businesses would originate and fewer still could grow as rapidly as their markets allow without the use of credit. This is particularly true of small companies that provide so many of our jobs, products and services. A parallel can be drawn between business loans and mortgage loans. Few Americans could buy homes if they could not borrow, and few businesses would originate or expand without credit. Our economy would be smaller without business credit, fewer products and services would be available, and fewer jobs would exist.

INTEREST RATES IN THE ECONOMY

The movements of short- and long-term interest rates command more attention than any other economic variable. The generally high level of interest rates is blamed for many of the economic ills which

Figure 1-1. Long-Term and Short-Term Corporate Liabilities Compared

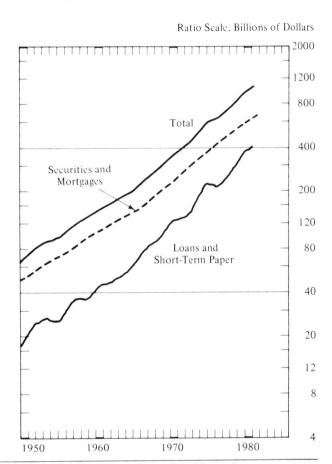

Ratio Scale, Billions of Dollars

Source: *1981 Historical Chart Book*, Federal Reserve System

the American people have encountered in recent years. While interest rates are the cause of problems in many respects, it also will be seen that they are the result of other problems in the economy.

There are many different interest rates in the economy, some of which are administered (set by regulation or the periodic decisions of an authoritative body) and some of which are determined by the free interaction of market forces. With few exceptions, administered rates are changed from time to time to bring them into line with, or at least closer to, rates determined by free market forces.

ADMINISTERED INTEREST RATES

Three examples of administered interest rates are: the discount rate, the prime rate and mortgage rates set by the Federal Housing Administration and the Veterans Administration.

Discount Rate

The Federal Reserve requires financial intermediaries to set aside reserves based on their deposits. The Federal Reserve Banks make loans to these intermediaries for the purpose of bringing reserve balances up to required levels. The loans are very short-term, usually for a day or a weekend. The rate charged by the Fed for these loans is called the discount rate. The Fed adjusts the discount rate from time to time in order to control credit.

Prime Rate

Each commercial bank has a rate which it charges on loans to its best borrowers. This rate is the bank's prime rate. Because of competition, the rate is the same, or very nearly so, at all commercial banks at any given time. Therefore, it is common to refer to "the prime" as though there were only one. Big banks are usually the trend setters, with smaller banks following along. When market rates of interest are experiencing rapid change, and banks are making frequent adjustments in their prime rates, there may be 1/4 or 1/2 point difference between large banks' prime rates, but this is usually temporary. Although the prime does not directly determine rates other than those on business loans, changes in the prime signify the direction other rates can be expected to take.

FHA and VA Mortgage Rates

Rates on Federal Housing Administration insured and Veterans Administration guaranteed mortgage loans are set by those bodies from time to time in response to changes in market-determined mortgage rates. Frequently, and particularly in periods of rising rates, the FHA and VA rates are lower than conventional mortgage rates, thus requiring lenders to compensate for the difference by charging what are termed discount points.[1]

MARKET INTEREST RATES

Four examples of market interest rates are: the federal funds rate, Treasury bill rates, commercial paper rates and bond yields.

---

[1] Marshall W. Dennis, *Mortgage Lending Fundamentals and Practices* (Reston, VA: Reston Publishing Co., 1981), p. 122.

Federal Funds Rate

Financial intermediaries which are required to maintain reserves at the Federal Reserve often have more reserves in their accounts than required. Others may have insufficient balances but are reluctant to borrow from the Fed. The Fed looks askance at too-frequent borrowing through the discount window. Thus, an intermediary in need of additional reserves may borrow the excess reserves of another intermediary. The rate paid for these overnight loans is called the federal funds rate. It is the most volatile rate in the economy, moving in wide swings almost every day in response to changes in the demand for and supply of reserve balances.

Treasury Bill Rates

Each week the U.S. Treasury auctions one or more new series of Treasury bills. The bills are issued with maturity dates of either 3, 6 or 12 months. Once they are issued, bills trade actively in the secondary market.[2] Interest rates on Treasury bills are determined by market forces, primarily supply and demand. For example, if the Treasury must borrow an unusually large amount at the T-bill auction one week, it would be expected that the rate paid by the Treasury would be higher than the previous week, all else being equal.

Treasury bill rates are very significant to the economy. First, the U.S. Treasury is considered the best of all borrowers in terms of credit risk. Second, the Treasury does a large amount of borrowing by selling bills, so a large supply of T-bills is always available to meet the short-term investment needs of individuals and organizations. Due to this pivotal position, the rate for six-month T-bills is used to set ceiling rates on the Money Market Certificates and Small Savers Certificates issued by financial intermediaries.

Commercial Paper Rates

Large corporations with strong credit ratings borrow large amounts of money for periods ranging from a week or less up to 270 days by issuing commercial paper. There is no pledge of collateral by the corporations. Thus, commercial paper is unsecured. Investors (lenders) include other corporations, financial intermediaries, and any individual or organization which may have temporarily idle funds in sizable amounts. Normally, the commercial paper market is considered an institutional market.

---

[2] Securities, like other assets, are first sold "new" and thereafter they are sold "used." New securities are said to be sold in the primary market and thereafter are sold in the secondary market.

Bond Yields

Bonds are long-term debt instruments, maturing in some cases as much as forty years from the date of issue. Bonds are issued by corporations, the federal government, and state and local governments. The yield on a bond is the average annual rate of return which an investor would earn from time of purchase to maturity date. Purchase may be in either the primary or secondary market.

INTEREST RATES OVER TIME

Interest rates have changed dramatically from time to time, particularly in recent years when sharp increases have been experienced. Figures 1-2, 1-3 and 1-4 show several of the more important interest rates over the last four decades.

SHORT-TERM AND LONG-TERM RATES

Figure 1-2 illustrates an important feature of interest rates, namely, short-term rates experience greater changes or swings than long-term rates. Financial instruments maturing in one year or less are considered short-term. Because short-term rates are sometimes higher and sometimes lower than long-term rates, it is not enough just to know that rates are "high" or "low." The person involved in commercial lending should be aware at all times of the relationship between short-term and long-term rates. The best way to do this is to master the concept of the yield curve.

YIELD CURVE

Various interest rates differ from one another because of degrees of risk, contractual variations, geographical influences, and differences between maturity or due dates. The purpose of the yield curve is to isolate yield differences due to maturity differences.

The yield curve depicts the interest rate structure at a specific point in time. It is a shorthand way to picture all of the rates in the economy by considering the shape of one curve. The yield curve is a useful tool in financial decision-making, including making commercial loans.

Figure 1-2. Long-Term and Short-Term Interest Rates Compared

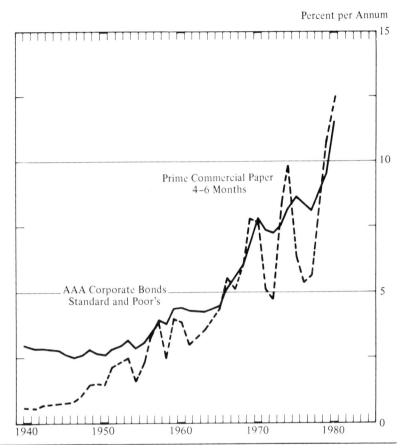

Source: *1981 Historical Chart Book*, Federal Reserve System

CONSTRUCTING A YIELD CURVE

Once the concept of the yield curve is mastered, its shape can be estimated at any time simply by glancing at a chart of interest rates such as the one in Figure 1-2. Another method is looking at the rates of return for U.S. Treasury securities published daily in *The Wall Street Journal* and the financial sections of major newspapers.

Figure 1-3. Three Short-Term Interest Rates Compared

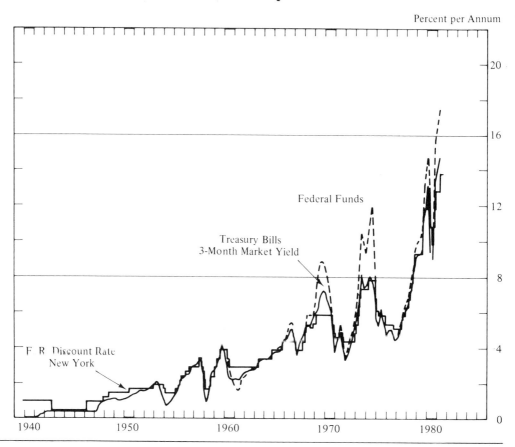

Source: *1981 Historical Chart Book*, Federal Reserve System

Constructing a yield curve usually is based on the rates of return available on U.S. Treasury securities. This is because there are so many issues of Treasury securities outstanding with maturities falling in virtually every year up to and including the year 2010, and because the rates available are the purest of freely determined market rates. This "purity" derives from the fact that the U.S. government is considered the most credit-worthy borrower in the world, and also because there is a vast free market for Treasury issues which is active every business day.

Figure 1-4. Commercial Paper Rate and Prime Rates Compared

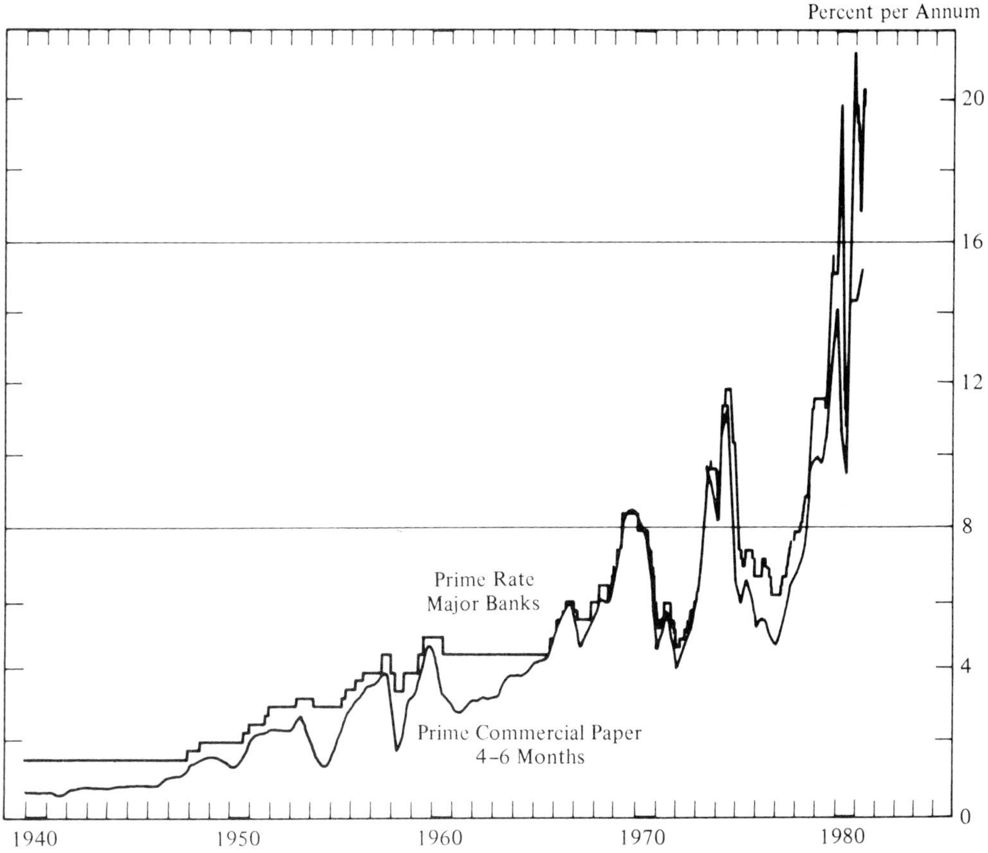

Source: *1981 Historical Chart Book*, Federal Reserve System

Figure 1-5 lists the Treasury bonds outstanding at the end of July 1980. The Treasury also issues bills (defined earlier in the chapter) and notes. Notes are issued with maturities from one to seven years while bonds are usually issued with maturities between seven and twenty years. The list of bonds in Figure 1-5 is sufficient to demonstrate construction of the yield curve.

The Treasury had 41 bond issues outstanding at the end of July 1980. The first bond in Figure 1-5 was originally issued October 3, 1960. It was issued with a 3-1/2 percent interest rate (this is called the coupon

Figure 1-5. Treasury Bond Quotations, July 31, 1980

(Price decimals are 32nds)

Description		Price		Yield		Issue date
		Bid	Change from last month	To first call or maturity	Change from last month	
3 1/6% –	11/15/80	98.13	+0.05	9.11%	+0.80%	10/03/60
7 –	8/15/81	97.28	−0.12	9.19	+0.52	8/15/71
6 3/8 –	2/15/82	95.12	−0.26	9.68	+0.73	2/15/72
3 1/4 –	6/15/78–83	86.26	−0.28	8.52	+0.51	5/01/53
6 3/8 –	8/15/84	88.02	−2.00	10.04	+0.71	8/15/72
3 1/4 –	5/15/85	86.13	−0.15	6.61	+0.18	6/03/58
4 1/4 –	5/15/75–85	86.21	−0.01	7.63	+0.06	4/15/60
6 1/8 –	11/15/86	83.24	−1.22	9.63	+0.44	11/15/71
3 1/2 –	2/15/90	86.14	−0.08	5.33	+0.05	2/14/58
8 1/4 –	5/15/90	87.10	−4.22	10.34	+0.82	4/07/75
4 1/4 –	8/15/87–92	87.02	−0.17	5.75	+0.07	8/15/62
7 1/4 –	8/15/92	78.00	−2.28	10.51	+0.50	7/08/77
4 –	2/15/88–93	87.02	+0.16	5.44	−0.05	1/17/63
6 3/4 –	2/15/93	77.16	−3.10	9.93	+0.56	1/10/73
7 7/8 –	2/15/93	80.20	−3.22	10.72	+0.62	1/06/78
7 1/2 –	8/15/88–93	77.30	−3.22	10.67	+0.62	8/15/73
8 5/8 –	8/15/93	84.14	−3.30	10.89	+0.63	7/11/78
8 5/8 –	11/15/93	84.12	−1.04	10.87	+0.65	10/10/78
9	2/15/94	86.25	−4.45	10.89	+0.69	1/11/79
4 1/8 –	5/15/89–94	87.08	+0.20	5.45	−0.07	4/18/63
8 3/4 –	8/15/94	84.28	−4.00	10.88	+0.62	7/09/79
10 1/8 –	11/15/94	94.14	−4.26	10.90	+0.67	10/18/79
3 –	2/15/95	87.02	+0.08	4.20	−0.02	2/15/55
10 1/2 –	2/15/95	97.06	−4.18	10.92	+0.63	1/10/80
10 3/8 –	5/15/95	96.02	−−	10.92	−−	7/09/80
12 5/8 –	5/15/95	110.10	−6.08	11.18	+0.77	4/08/80
7 –	5/15/93–98	71.03	−5.19	10.66	+0.87	5/15/73
3 1/2 –	11/15/98	87.00	+0.16	4.56	−0.04	10/03/60
8 1/2 –	5/15/94–99	82.16	−4.20	10.68	+0.65	2/18/74
7 7/8 –	2/15/95–00	76.16	−4.22	10.78	+0.68	2/18/75
8 3/8 –	8/15/95–00	80.14	−4.16	10.78	+0.64	8/15/75
8 –	8/15/95–00	76.30	−4.28	10.80	+0.70	8/16/76
8 1/4 –	5/15/00–05	78.14	−4.28	10.76	+0.67	5/15/75
7 5/8 –	2/15/02–07	74.04	−4.08	10.54	+0.59	2/15/77
7 7/8 –	11/15/02–07	77.02	−3.04	10.43	+0.43	11/15/77
8 3/8 –	8/15/03–08	79.24	−4.20	10.66	+0.63	8/15/78
8 3/4 –	11/15/03–08	82.28	−5.04	10.68	+0.65	11/15/78
9 1/8 –	5/15/04–09	86.08	−5.14	10.67	+0.66	5/15/79
10 3/8 –	11/15/04–09	96.08	−6.14	10.80	+0.71	11/15/79
11 3/4 –	2/15/05–10	106.22	−7.06	10.96	+0.76	2/15/80
10 –	5/15/05–10	93.30	−6.04	10.68	+0.69	5/15/80

Source: *The Treasury Bulletin*, August 1980

rate). This was the market rate of interest for government bonds at that time. The bond was scheduled to mature November 15, 1980, just 3-1/2 months after the July 31, 1980 date of the list.

Under the price heading in Figure 1-5 it should be noted that the bid (what someone was willing to pay for the bond on November 15, 1980) was 98.13. Government bonds are quoted in whole numbers and 32nds, so the bid was 98 and 13/32. A buyer of the bonds with $10,000 face amount would have paid $9,840.63. If purchased at that price and held until the maturity date, the buyer would have earned the difference between the purchase price and $10,000, or $159.37 + 3-1/2 percent on 10,000 for 3-1/2 months. These two amounts added together would produce an annual rate, or yield, of 9.11 percent on the amount invested. This is shown in the first column under yield. The yields for all the Treasury bonds in Figure 1-5 plus those for bills and notes were used to construct the yield curve shown in Figure 1-6.

The curve is prepared by first plotting points that correspond to the intersection of the yield (vertical axis) and maturity date (horizontal axis) for each bond, note and bill. Then a line is drawn which best represents all of the plotted points. The line is the yield curve for July 31, 1980.

THE MEANING AND USE OF THE YIELD CURVE

Investors accept lower yields when they buy Treasury securities than when they buy corporate issues of similar maturity, because the Treasury is the strongest of all creditors. Thus, the yield curve for Treasury securities reflects lower yields than would a curve that was based on corporate bond yields.

The yield curve represents the basic rate structure in the economy. If the people involved in commercial lending have in mind the shape and level of the curve, they will be able to understand and explain rates applicable to various forms of loans, the cost of funds to the institution and many other considerations related to interest rates.

COMPARING YIELD CURVES

The July 31, 1980, curve gives an example of what many economists refer to as the "normal" yield curve. It is considered normal because it reflects a yield structure which one might normally expect; yields on shorter maturity instruments are lower than those on longer maturities. This seems reasonable because there is more uncertainty associated with the more distant maturity dates than with those close

Figure 1-6. Yield Curve of Treasury Securities, July 31, 1980

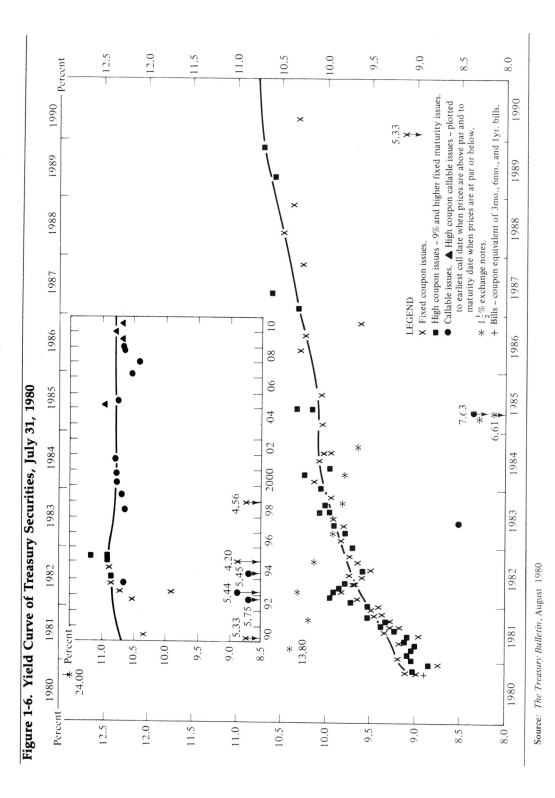

Source: *The Treasury Bulletin,* August 1980

at hand. There are times, however, and this has been particularly true since the early 1970s, when the normal yield curve does not prevail.

Figure 1-7 shows the curve for September 30, 1981. This curve has an "inverted" shape, that is, short-term rates are higher than long-term rates except for a few of the very shortest issues. Also, interest rates in general were much higher on September 30, 1981, than on July 31, 1980.

The shape as well as the level of the yield curve can be very important in the commercial lending process, in deciding whether or not a loan can be made, and if so, how it should be structured. The shape and level of the curve also will influence the income and expenses of many businesses as well as affecting the cost and availability of funds to financial institutions.

INFLUENCES ON INTEREST RATES

There is a great deal of disagreement as to the degree to which certain factors influence the level of interest rates and the shape of the yield curve. Many theories abound and economists are in constant disagreement. The commercial loan officer cannot spend the time necessary to evaluate all the arguments, but still he or she must be able to think about and converse about the major factors which influence interest rates.

It is convenient to think of interest rate influences as falling into two categories: what is presently happening and what is expected to happen. The influences in the first category affect supply and demand. Since the interest rate is the price of money, like other prices it moves up and down due to supply and demand forces. The primary factors influencing supply and demand at any time are economic conditions, government borrowing and Federal Reserve monetary policy.

ECONOMIC CONDITIONS

When the economy is strong, individuals and businesses are likely to be heavy borrowers, putting upward pressure on interest rates. Individuals borrow to buy homes and other long-term assets as well as to take vacations, pay for education, and for other nontangible and current consumption purposes. Businesses borrow to buy raw materials and other types of inventory items, and pay expenses in order to produce or otherwise obtain the products necessary to meet the high level of demand from a strong economy. When the economy turns

Figure 1-7. Yield Curve of Treasury Securities, September 30, 1981

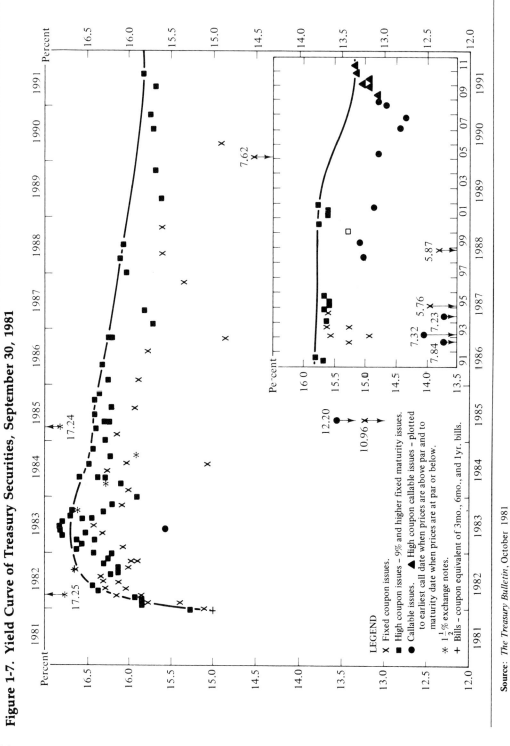

LEGEND
X Fixed coupon issues.
■ High coupon issues – 9% and higher fixed maturity issues.
● Callable issues. ▲ High coupon callable issues – plotted to earliest call date when prices are above par and to maturity date when prices are at par or below.
* $1\frac{1}{2}$% exchange notes.
+ Bills – coupon equivalent of 3mo., 6mo., and 1yr. bills.

Source: *The Treasury Bulletin*, October 1981

down, into recession, many individuals curtail their expenditures, thus cutting their demand for credit and perhaps even reducing existing debt. Businesses suddenly find themselves with excessive inventories, so they stop borrowing and also reduce some of their debt as they gradually sell off their inventories. The reduced demand for credit by individuals and businesses is an influence toward lower interest rates.[3]

GOVERNMENT BORROWING

Borrowing by the federal, state and local governments has been heavy in recent years. State and local governments usually borrow on a long-term basis to construct schools and other facilities. The federal government in recent years has incurred huge deficits, that is, its revenues from taxes and other sources have fallen far short of its expenditures. Its borrowings are primarily for current purposes. Government borrowing puts upward pressure on interest rates. It may be heaviest during recessions because the personal and corporate income tax revenues on which the federal government in particular is so dependent may be depressed due to unemployment and reduced business sales.

The federal government, through the efforts of the president and the Congress, attempts to influence the economy through expenditures (the budget) and receipts (taxes). This is called fiscal policy. Fiscal policy in recent years is considered by many to have had an upward influence on interest rates because of intentional deficits. In addition, the deficits have in most years been larger than projected. This means that the federal government has been a continuous and major borrower in the money and capital markets, competing with the borrowing needs of individuals and businesses; helping to drive up interest rates.[4]

FEDERAL RESERVE MONETARY POLICY

The Federal Reserve is the regulatory body charged with management of the money supply. How it chooses to influence the money

---

[3] Anyone involved in commercial lending should make certain that his or her basic understanding of economics is intact. For anyone who has not had the benefit of a course of study in economics, a review of a basic economics text is recommended. See for example, Campbell R. McConnell, *Economics*, 7th edition (New York, NY: McGraw-Hill Book Company, 1978).

[4] The money market is that portion of financial market activity in which short-term instruments such as Treasury bills and commercial paper are traded. The capital market includes the trading of long-term debt and equity instruments.

supply is termed monetary policy. In addition, the Fed is the primary regulator of commercial banks and also administers Regulation D, which controls the reserve requirements of all depository institutions. Besides these functions the Fed maintains a check-clearing system and serves other regulatory functions.[5]

Money Supply Defined

Economists have numerous definitions of money, ranging from a narrow definition to various broader definitions. These can be found in the monthly editions of the *Federal Reserve Bulletin*. The purpose here is not to discuss the arguments for and against the various definitions, but rather to gain a feeling for the Fed's influence on interest rates through its monetary policy. For that purpose, the narrowly defined money supply, called M1, will be used. By this definition money consists of currency and coin held by the public, all demand deposits and NOW accounts at depository institutions, and traveler's checks.

This definition is comfortable if money is thought of as being that which can be spent directly without the need for an intermediate conversion process. An individual may make payment at the grocery store with cash by drawing on his or her NOW or checking account, or by use of a traveler's check. Broader definitions of money (M2, etc.) include assets such as passbook savings accounts which must be converted to cash or to demand deposits or to NOW accounts before they can be spent.

At the end of 1981, M1 totalled $441 billion. Of that amount, $123 billion was currency, $4 billion was traveler's checks and the balance ($314 billion) was demand deposits and NOW accounts.

Implementing Monetary Policy

The Federal Reserve, through the exercise of its monetary policy instruments, has the ability to influence the rate at which the money supply grows. Its influence in the short run is far from perfect, but over longer periods of time it is the Fed's monetary policy that largely determines the growth rate of the money supply. If it follows a "tight" monetary policy, the money supply grows slowly, if at all, and the supply of funds available to borrowers is restricted. This exerts upward pressure on interest rates. The opposite effects result when an "easy" monetary policy is followed. It should be stressed, however, that these are short-term effects. (Long-term effects are suggested later in th chapter.)

---

[5] *Introduction to the Savings Association Business*, 3rd edition (Chicago, IL: The Institute of Financial Education, 1979), Ch. 7.

The Federal Reserve has three monetary policy tools: the reserve requirement, the discount rate and open market operations. If the Fed wants to impose a tighter monetary policy, it can increase the amount of reserves which depository institutions are required to maintain. This reduces the funds available for lending. Also, the Fed can raise the discount rate. This discourages financial institutions from borrowing from the Fed to meet deficiencies in their reserves. Financial institutions will be more likely to reduce their lending activities than pay the higher discount rate. The reduction in loans available tends to have an upward effect on interest rates if borrowing demand does not decline.

Open market operations refers to the purchase and sale by the Fed of U.S. government securities in the open market. This is the most frequently used monetary policy tool, with open market purchases and sales taking place almost daily.

If the Fed wants to tighten monetary policy through open market operations, it offers to sell government securities to any of several large banks or bond dealers. If a bank buys the securities, it pays the Fed by having its deposits (reserves) at the Fed reduced. If the securities are bought by a bond dealer, the dealer pays the Fed with a check drawn on a bank, and the Fed deducts this amount from that bank's deposits. In either case, bank reserves are reduced and the funds available for lending to the public decline. With fewer funds available for lending, interest rates should be expected to rise.[6]

Why would the Fed want to impose a tight monetary policy that would exert upward pressure on interest rates and increase interest expenses for Americans and their institutions? The main reason is to fight inflation.

ROLE OF INFLATION

Earlier it was stated that it is convenient to think about the factors that influence interest rates as falling into one of two categories: what is presently happening and what is expected to happen. The second category, anticipated inflation, is by far the more important factor.

Inflation–the general increase in the prices of goods and services and decline in the purchasing power of the dollar–has been present

---

[6] All of the monetary policy tools work in the other direction if the Fed decides to ease monetary policy. It can lower reserve requirements, reduce the discount rate or buy government securities in the open market. If the Fed buys securities from a bank, it simply adds the amount to that bank's reserves. If it buys from a bond dealer, the check it gives the dealer is deposited in a bank and when it reaches the Fed is added to that bank's reserves.

to some degree since the end of World War II. However, the rate of inflation has increased since the late 1960s, as shown in Figure 1-8.

If Americans expect a high rate of inflation to continue, those who have money to lend or invest will adjust upwards the rate of return they require in order to try to offset the loss of purchasing power to inflation. For example, if an inflation rate of ten percent is anticipated, lenders attempt to get a return somewhat above ten percent, say thirteen percent. If inflation was expected to be only three percent, lenders might be satisfied with a return of six percent.

What causes inflation? Most economists consider the primary cause of inflation to be growth in the money supply that is too rapid in relationship to the growth of the supply of goods and services. Therefore, if a high rate of inflation exists in the present period, it is presumably due to excessive money supply growth in past periods.

A dilemma appears to arise that points up the difficulty of forecasting interest rate levels or movements. It was pointed out previously that the Fed would impose a tight monetary policy to fight inflation. Too much money in the economy is considered the primary cause of inflation. However, a tight monetary policy puts upward pressure on interest rates. If, on the other hand, an easy monetary policy is followed, inflation will increase and so will expectations of high future rates of inflation. Presumably, interest rates will rise as the result of the easy monetary policy. The dilemma is resolved–in the mind and perhaps in practice–by recognizing that though a tight money policy may push interest rates up in the short term, it should bring rates down in the long term as the policy works to slow money supply growth and reduce inflation. Lower actual rates of inflation should produce expectations of lower future rates of inflation and help bring interest rates down.

A tight monetary policy slows the economy, however, since less borrowing means lower sales for businesses, less production and higher rates of unemployment. A tight monetary policy can bring about a recession and, at times, fear of a depression.[7] Therefore, the Fed must be cognizant of the potential for causing recession when it applies a tight monetary policy to fight inflation and periodically reports to Congress on the rate of monetary growth it intends to attempt to bring about. For example, the target for M1 for 1982 was set at 2-1/2 to 5-1/2 percent.

---

[7] A recession is a period usually no longer than a few months in which production and employment decline moderately. A depression is a long period of severe decline in production, employment and consumer purchases. In a depression, businesses suffer so much damage that many fail, making economic recovery extremely difficult.

Figure 1-8. Consumer Prices: Food Compared to All Items, 1940-1980

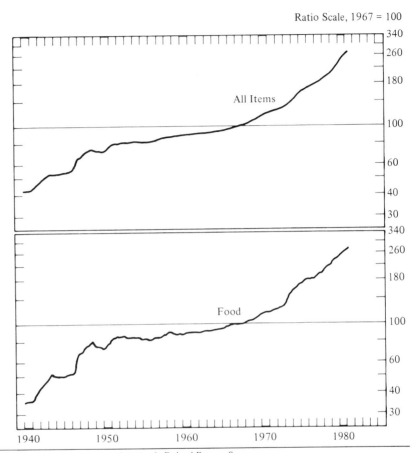

Source: *1981 Historical Chart Book*, Federal Reserve System

MONETARY POLICY VERSUS FISCAL POLICY

The Federal Reserve is independent of both the president and Congress in the formation of its monetary policy. Members of the Board of Governors of the Federal Reserve System are appointed by the president, but their terms are for 14 years. Thus, a new president inherits a board whose members were appointed by past presidents.

As a result of its independence, there are times when the Fed's monetary policy is in conflict with fiscal policy. For example, fiscal policy might be directed to stimulate the economy through a cut in individual income taxes resulting in a budget deficit. Presumably the tax cut would encourage individuals to spend more, helping accelerate overall economic activity. If, however, the Fed viewed the tax cut and resultant deficit as potentially inflationary, it might maintain a tight monetary policy which would have the effect of defeating the intent of the tax cut.

SOURCES OF COMMERCIAL LOANS

COMMERCIAL BANKS

The commercial banking system is the dominant financial intermediary in commercial lending. Commercial banks are so named because their primary function for so many years was to finance commerce. Commercial banks' specialization in commercial lending in the early nineteenth century, as well as their general unwillingness to accept savings deposits, left unsatisfied the needs which led to the formation of what are now savings and loan associations and mutual savings banks. The first mutual savings bank in the United States was formed shortly after the War of 1812. The forerunner of today's savings and loan associations, the Oxford Provident Building Association, was organized in 1831.[8]

Although they were generally unwilling to accept interest bearing deposits, commercial banks did take deposits which could be transferred by written order. This process developed into checking account banking which came into wide use in the late nineteenth century. Until recent years, commercial banks had a monopoly on demand deposits, that is, the deposits underlying checking accounts. Since commercial banks could not pay interest on demand deposit balances (law was passed in the 1930s forbidding such interest payments), the only costs connected to these balances were processing costs.

Demand deposit balances comprised a major portion of commercial bank funds for many years. While this continues to be true, the relative amount of funds provided to commercial banks in the form of demand deposit balances has declined dramatically in the last few years. For example, as of the end of 1976, demand deposits made up 41 percent of total commercial bank deposits, while at the end of 1981 this

---

[8] *Introduction to the Savings Association Business,* 3rd edition (Chicago, IL: The Institute of Financial Education, 1979), pp. 2-12.

figure was 29 percent. This decline is in part due to the expanded use of NOW accounts and related types of accounts at savings associations and other depository institutions, but it is also the result of the very high interest rates of recent years. These high rates have encouraged individuals and businesses to keep temporary funds in such short-term, high yielding assets as Treasury bills and money market funds.[9]

Commercial banks did not enter into real estate and consumer lending to any significant degree until the 1920s and 1930s. These are not important aspects of commercial bank business. In addition, commercial banks provide many other services, including equipment and real property leasing, safe deposit services, trust services, credit cards, data processing services, foreign exchange and underwriting bond issues of municipalities. Of course, not every bank offers every service and the largest, either directly or through subsidiaries, may be engaged in numerous activities not mentioned here.

The diversification of deposit forms, services and types of loans has been valuable to commercial banks. They have not suffered the declines in profits nor the loss of asset values that rising interest rates have brought to other financial institutions since 1978. In Chapter 2 the harmful effects of rising interest rates will be illustrated.

Figure 1-9 provides a comparison of commercial banks with savings associations in terms of major categories of assets and liabilities. It also shows that commercial banks have assets totaling approximately three times those of savings associations. With approximately $400 billion in commercial loans in their portfolios and their many locations, commercial banking's dominance in commercial lending is obvious. However, by no means does all of the credit supplied to business come from commercial banks.

OTHER SOURCES OF COMMERCIAL CREDIT

Businesses obtain credit from many sources. Some sources specialize in particular types of credit and others are more general. The more well-known sources are described below.

---

[9] Money market funds, offered primarily by investment firms and insurance companies, are pooled types of investments. The monies of many individuals and businesses are pooled and the funds invested in high quality, short-term assets such as Treasury bills, the commercial paper of large corporations and large-denomination certificates of deposit. Money can be withdrawn from money market funds at any time by check, and thus they serve as close substitutes for commercial bank checking accounts while paying market rates of interest.

Figure 1-9.   Commercial Banks and Savings Associations, Assets and Liabilities, As of December 31, 1981

Assets	Commercial Banks		Savings Associations	
Cash and Securities	$ 532	29%	$ 62	9%
Commercial Loans	407	23	– –	– –
Mortgage Loans	286	16	518	78
Consumer Loans	210	12	– –	– –
Other Assets	370	20	82	13
	$1,805	100%	$ 662	100%
Liabilities and Net Worth				
Demand Deposits	$ 378	21%	$ – –	– –%
Savings	910	50	524	80
Borrowings	251	14	89	13
Other Liabilities	136	8	21	3
Net Worth	130	7	28	4
	$1,805	100%	$ 662	100%

Source: *Federal Reserve Bulletin*, February 1982

Money and Capital Markets

Large corporations are able to borrow by selling their bonds and notes in the open market, usually through an underwriting process conducted by investment firms. Financially strong corporations are also able to borrow large amounts through the issuance of commercial paper.

Suppliers

Many of the companies that sell their products to other companies provide terms for payment, that is they might allow the purchaser 30 or 60 days before payment is due. This type of lending is called trade credit and is an important source of credit for many firms, particularly small ones.

Insurance Companies

Some of the long-term credit needs of business are met by insurance companies. Besides stressing long-term loans, insurance companies usually limit their lending to large companies. Lending directly to business is not a major activity of the insurance industry, however, with business loans probably comprising only two or three percent of insurance company assets.

Finance Companies

The group of financial intermediaries known as finance companies lend to consumers and business. Some finance companies specialize in a particular area, but in recent years many finance companies, particularly the larger ones, have made credit available both to consumers and business. Finance companies which lend to business make virtually all forms of credit available, either long- or short-term, and may also lease assets to business and provide factoring services. *Factoring* is the purchase of accounts receivable as opposed to accepting them as collateral for loans.

Leasing Companies

Leasing is equivalent to intermediate-term lending and will be discussed in Chapter 5. Although a few companies specialize in leasing, it is a sideline for many others.

Federal Government Agencies

The Small Business Administration, the Farmers Home Administration and other federal government agencies provide some direct credit to business. Usually these organizations prefer to provide guarantees for loans made by private financial intermediaries.

Savings Associations

Businesses have received mortgage financing and construction loans from savings associations for many years. Associations also provide inventory for mobile home dealers and, in states where regulation allows, state-chartered associations make other forms of business loans. In addition, service corporations owned by savings associations are authorized to make various forms of business loans. These include inventory loans to dealers on goods used for personal or household purposes; loans to alter, repair, improve or furnish business properties; and certain other business loans secured at least in part by real estate. They may also make certain business loans that are insured or guaranteed by an agency of the U.S. government.

Mutual Savings Banks

Federally chartered mutual savings banks have authority to make business loans. Such loans can comprise no more than five percent of total assets and must be made only within a bank's home state or within 75 miles of its home office. This authority was granted by the Depository Institutions Deregulation and Monetary Control Act of 1980, signed by President Carter on March 31, 1980.

Individuals

Small businesses many times borrow from relatives or close friends. These loans are not always based on sound credit analysis, yet the borrower may feel more compulsion to repay a friend or relative than a loan from a financial intermediary. Ultimately, all credit comes from individuals, because it is their deposits, the deposits of the businesses they own, their insurance premiums and investments in financial intermediaries that provide the funds for commercial loans.

SUMMARY

The environment of commercial lending is largely defined by economic considerations and the various competitors involved in commercial lending. The person who becomes involved in commercial lending should develop a good understanding of these economic and competitive elements.

First, the commercial loan officer should appreciate the importance of commercial lending to the economy. Second, of all the economic influences, by far the most important is interest rates and their impact on commercial lending. The commercial lending officer should be aware of the level and recent direction of rates, know the difference between administered and market determined rates, understand the meaning of the yield curve and know the important factors that influence interest rates.

The Federal Reserve System, how it conducts monetary policy and the influence of the Fed on the nation's money supply should be topics of study for anyone in commercial lending. The conflict between short-term and long-term objectives of monetary policy and on occasion between monetary policy and fiscal policy should be appreciated.

Credit to business comes from many sources. The most important of these is the commercial banking system. With its huge size and large number of outlets, the commercial banking system largely defines the competitive environment of commercial banking.

CHAPTER QUESTIONS

1. Why is commercial lending important to the economy?
2. What is the prime rate and how is it determined?

3. Which category of interest rates is more volatile: long-term or short-term? Explain why.

4. Why is the yield curve important to financial decision makers?

5. What is monetary policy? Who conducts monetary policy in the United States?

6. What is fiscal policy and how may it be in conflict with monetary policy from time to time?

7. Which financial intermediary is dominant in the area of commercial lending? Explain how this dominance influenced the emergence of other financial intermediaries.

2

Basic
Financial Considerations

OBJECTIVES

After reading Chapter 2, you should be able to:

- Describe the purpose and makeup of the balance sheet and the income statement;
- Describe the purpose and makeup of the sources and uses of funds statement;
- List the important asset, liability and income statement entries;
- State the importance of the audit and footnotes in financial statement preparation;
- Explain the concept of cash flow;
- Define depreciation, liquidity and leverage;
- Illustrate the negative effect of rising interest rates;
- Cite three basic interest rate concepts.

FINANCIAL STATEMENTS

Business firms prepare financial reports at the end of specified periods, particularly at year-end.[1] The most important reports are the balance sheet, income statement, and sources and uses of funds statement.[2]

BALANCE SHEET

The *balance sheet* shows the financial condition of the firm at a particular point in time, for example, at the close of business on December 31. It is often compared with a photograph of the firm, in financial terms, at a particular point in time. The balance sheet is divided into two parts, the totals of which are equal; thus the name "balance sheet." Although these two parts are not necessarily presented side-by-side, it helps in thinking about the two parts if they are considered as the left side and the right side.

The left side of the balance sheet lists the firm's assets, that is, what it has to use to conduct its business. On the right side are listed its liabilities–what it owes–and the owner's equity (net worth). A conceptual way to think about the balance sheet is that the right side shows the funds' sources–debt or owner's equity–that provided the dollars to acquire the assets listed on the left side. Thus, the two sides must be equal, and:

$$\text{Assets} = \text{Liabilities} + \text{Owner's Equity}$$

is the basic accounting equation. This equation will be used to develop the balance sheet for a new retail business.

Mr. Jones Starts a Business

Mr. Jones decided to open a men's clothing store. He wanted to open for business on January 2, which was less than three months away. He had $150,000 cash which he put into a checking account under the business name, Jones Store for Men. At that point, if a

---

[1] Because of seasonal or other influences, many firms report on a fiscal year basis which differs from the calendar year. The fiscal year would be the twelve-month period ending on the last day of any month (except December) that the firm considers most appropriate.

[2] All of these statements may be found with other titles. For example, the balance sheet is often called statement of financial position, the income statement may be termed the profit and loss statement, and the sources and uses of funds statement also goes under names such as statement of changes in financial position or funds flow statement.

balance sheet had been drawn up, it would have appeared as follows:[3]

JONES STORE FOR MEN
Balance Sheet - October 31, 198A

Assets		Liabilities and Owner's Equity	
Cash	$150,000	Paid in Capital	$150,000
Total	$150,000	Total	$150,000

Next, after a short search, Mr. Jones located a store building, that he purchased outright for $100,000. He also bought a $40,000 inventory of men's clothing from a wholesaler. If a new balance sheet had been prepared at that point in time, it would have appeared as follows:

JONES STORE FOR MEN
Balance Sheet - November 15, 198A

Assets		Liabilities and Owner's Equity	
Current Assets			
Cash	$10,000		
Inventory	40,000		
Fixed Assets			
Building	100,000	Paid in Capital	$150,000
Total	$150,000	Total	$150,000

While the makeup of Mr. Jones' assets changed, their dollar total did not, because nothing changed on the right side of the balance sheet. Also, note that two categories of assets now exist; current assets and fixed assets. *Current assets* are defined as cash plus other assets which are expected to be converted to cash in a short time, usually in the normal course of business. *Fixed assets* are long-term in nature, are used in the operation of the business and usually are not sold as a part of normal business activity.

---

[3] This presentation intentionally avoids attempting accounting precision since the purpose here is to develop workable concepts. Individuals involved in commercial lending normally are more concerned with how to apply the statements in the lending process than with how the statements are prepared. However, additional study of basic accounting principles is recommended for those involved in commercial lending.

After Mr. Jones placed the $40,000 of inventory in the store, he decided that the inventory was not sufficient to begin business. He wanted to have a grand opening sale and felt the shelves and racks should be well stocked on opening day. From a financial intermediary he borrowed $50,000 and agreed to repay this loan in less than a year. With the money, he purchased additional inventory from the wholesaler. If a new balance sheet had been prepared, it would have been as follows:

JONES STORE FOR MEN
Balance Sheet - November 30, 198A

Assets		Liabilities and Owner's Equity	
Current Assets		Current Liabilities	
Cash	$10,000	Note Payable	$50,000
Inventory	90,000		
Fixed Assets			
Building	100,000	Paid in Capital	$150,000
Total	$200,000	Total	$200,000

Mr. Jones had more inventory at that point, but also a debt, a current liability. It was a current liability because he promised to pay it soon (in less than one year).

As Mr. Jones prepared for opening day, he became aware that most of the men in the area had sons, so he decided he should include a line of boys' clothing. He returned to the financial intermediary, obtained an additional $50,000 by mortgaging his building (for convenience this example ignores the time and complexity normally involved in a mortgage loan), and purchased $50,000 worth of boys' clothing. The balance sheet then looked like this:

JONES STORE FOR MEN
Balance Sheet - December 31, 198A

Assets		Liabilities and Owner's Equity	
Current Assets		Current Liabilities	
Cash	$ 10,000	Note Payable	$ 50,000
Inventory	140,000	Long-term Liabilities	
Fixed Assets		Mortgage	50,000
Building	100,000	Paid in Capital	$150,000
Total	$250,000	Total	$250,000

INCOME STATEMENT

While the balance sheet is often compared with a still photograph, the *income statement* resembles a motion picture. It shows the firm's activity for a particular period of time, that is, the period between the current balance sheet and the prior one. It lists the total dollar amount of sales during the period, deducts the expenses associated with those sales and ends with the profit (or loss) that results from the period's operations.

Mr. Jones' First Year

The previous balance sheet dated December 31 showed the status of Mr. Jones' business as he opened his doors on the first business day of January. On December 31, one year later, he prepared his income statement for his first year of business.

Throughout the year he had bought and sold many items of clothing, all at a markup from his cost. His sales totaled $300,000. The goods he sold cost him $200,000. However, Mr. Jones did not finish the year with a profit of $100,000. Through the year he incurred many expenses as a result of being in business, such as maintenance costs, heat, lighting, insurance and many others. These expenses totaled $50,000. Also, to meet his personal expenses, Mr. Jones had drawn a salary during the year totaling $20,000. Depreciation expense on the building, which will be explained in the next section, was $5,000.

In addition to these expenses, Mr. Jones paid interest of $10,000 on his loans. And, finally, income taxes were paid as a result of the profitable operation during the first year.[4] The income statement for the year is as follows:

JONES STORE FOR MEN
Income Statement - Year Ended December 31, 198B

<u>Sales</u>	
Sales	$300,000
<u>Cost of Goods Sold</u>	
Cost of goods sold	200,000
Gross margin on sales	$100,000

---

[4] Technically, whether or not income taxes are paid by the business and appear on the income statement depends on the form of business. If Mr. Jones operates the store as a proprietorship, then the store's profit before tax is added to any income he may have from other sources on his personal income tax return. His business, as such, pays no income tax. If, however, the business was organized as a corporation, it would be viewed as a separate legal entity and it would pay income tax. Forms of business organization are described in Chapter 8.

Operating Expenses

General expenses	$50,000	
Salary	20,000	
Depreciation	5,000	
Total operating expenses		$ 75,000
Income from operations		$ 25,000

Other Expenses

Interest expense	10,000
Income before taxes	$ 15,000
Income taxes (50%)	7,500
Net income	$ 7,500

The 50 percent tax is used only for illustrative purposes. If it is assumed Mr. Jones' business is incorporated, then the federal income tax rate applicable to the first $25,000 of income is 17 percent. If it is assumed he operated as a sole proprietorship, his income from other sources would have been sizable in order for him to impute a 50 percent tax rate to the $15,000 derived from the store. For convenience in developing other concepts, it will be assumed the store operates as a corporation and the applicable tax rate is 50 percent.

Depreciation

The depreciation expense shown on the previous income statement is an example of a noncash expense. This means that money did not actually flow out of the firm during the year as was the case when the heating and lighting bills were paid. The depreciation expense is charged against revenues to allocate amounts spent in the past for fixed assets to the several periods in which those assets will be used. Assume the life of the Jones' store building is considered to be 20 years. In this situation, the depreciation expense to be charged will be 1/20 of the cost, or $5,000 each year. This is the "straight line" method of charging depreciation. The Internal Revenue Service and state taxing authorities also allow "accelerated" methods which increase the amounts charged in the early years of an asset's life and reduce the charge in the later years.

It is well known that most economically useful buildings have been increasing in value in recent years rather than decreasing in value. Why then make a deduction for depreciation? Also, the depreciation expense charge reduced the book value of the building and decreased net worth, as the balance sheet below shows.[5] The reason for deducting depreciation is taxes, or rather tax savings. An examination of the previous income statement will make this clear. Without the depreciation expense, the income tax charge would have been $10,000 rather than $7,500.

Accounts Receivable and Accounts Payable

Many businesses attempt to increase sales by providing credit to customers. For many firms, competition makes this unavoidable. Allowing a customer to buy goods on credit results in a short-term asset called *accounts receivable*. Also, firms such as the Jones Store for Men often buy from suppliers on credit (trade credit was discussed in Chapter 1), and this temporary borrowing creates a current liability called *accounts payable*.

These credit transactions do not show on the income statement. Sales and cost of goods sold are the same whether sales were for cash or credit. It is just that short-term "promises to pay" were given to Mr. Jones for some goods sold and by Mr. Jones for some goods purchased. The balance sheet that follows, as of the end of Mr. Jones' first year of operation, shows that customers owe the store $10,000 at that point in time and the store owes suppliers $15,000. The depreciation charge of $5,000 is also shown as a reduction in the book value of the building.

JONES STORE FOR MEN
Balance Sheet - December 31, 198B

Assets		Liabilities and Owner's Equity	
Current Assets		Current Liabilities	
Cash	$ 5,000	Accounts Payable	$ 15,000
Accounts Receivable	10,000	Long-term Liabilities	
Inventory	107,500	Mortgage	45,000
Fixed Assets			
Building		Owner's Equity	
($100,000 less		Paid in Capital	150,000
accumulated		Retained Earnings	7,500
depreciation			
$5,000)	95,000		
Total	$217,500	Total	$217,500

---

[5] Book value of an asset is its original cost plus or minus any adjustments, such as a depreciation write-down. The balance sheet carries book values, but actual market values may be much more or much less. Commercial lenders must learn to look behind book values to judge the market or liquidating values of assets.

SOURCES AND USES OF FUNDS STATEMENT

The previous balance sheet is significantly changed from the balance sheet of one year earlier, just before Mr. Jones first opened for business. The income statement shows the net amount added to owner's equity as net income, that can be seen as the new balance sheet account, retained earnings. However, to analyze the movement or flow of funds within the firm that resulted in the changes observed on the most recent balance sheet, a sources and uses of funds statement is prepared. (For the purposes of this section "funds" is considered synonymous with cash.)

JONES STORE FOR MEN
Sources and Uses of Funds - Year Ended December 31, 198B

Sources of Funds		
Retained Earnings		$ 7,500
Depreciation		5,000
Decrease in cash		5,000
Decrease in inventory		32,500
	Total	$50,000
Uses of Funds		
Decrease in current liabilities		35,000
Decrease in long-term liabilities		5,000
Increase in accounts receivable		10,000
	Total	$50,000

The sources and uses statement allows one to determine where dollars were produced and where they were absorbed during the year. This process is called *funds flow analysis*, and it is useful to those involved in commercial lending when evaluating the financial health of a firm. In preparing the sources and uses statement, a *source* is a decrease in an asset, an increase in a liability or an increase in owner's equity (either by retention of earnings or from additions by owners). A *use* is an increase in an asset, a decrease in a liability or a decrease in owner's equity (either as a result of net losses from operations or withdrawals by owners).

What happened to Mr. Jones' business during the year from one balance sheet to the next? The sources and uses statement shows $50,000 was generated from four sources (earnings retained, depreciation expense charged, cash expended and inventory reduced). The $50,000 was utilized in three ways (to decrease current liabilities, decrease long-term liabilities and increase the asset, accounts receivable).

OTHER ASSET AND LIABILITY ACCOUNTS

Several other accounts will appear on balance sheets in addition to those described earlier. Some of the more important ones follow.

Prepaid Expenses

This is a current asset representing such items as real estate taxes and insurance premiums. If these were paid, for example, on November 30, and were not due again until the following November 30, the balance sheet prepared December 31 would show 11/12 of the payment as a current asset.

Goodwill

This asset item usually results when one company buys another company for more than the book value of the purchased company. The assets and liabilities of the purchased company are blended with those of the buyer, and since the excess over book value must be reflected in some manner, it goes to create an account called goodwill. It is referred to as an intangible asset, along with patents and copyrights. Commercial lenders usually reduce net worth by the amount of intangible assets when analyzing a balance sheet.

Notes Payable

This current liability may be owed to a financial intermediary or to a supplier. If it is owed to a supplier, it may exist because trade credit was not retired according to terms and the supplier has required a signed note in support of the obligation.

Accrued Expenses

This reflects current expenses where the benefits have been received but not yet paid for. It may include accrued taxes. If so, there should be some concern because the claims of taxing authorities take precedence over creditor's claims.

PREPARATION OF FINANCIAL STATEMENTS

Although persons involved in commercial lending need not be accountants, they do need to understand business financial statements and how these statements are prepared. Some statements give very incomplete information, and even those that are quite detailed may give very confusing impressions of the condition or performance of a company.

Statements of very small businesses may be prepared without the help of a professional accountant. In such cases, personal and business assets, liabilities, income and expenses may be so intermixed that financial analysis is largely an evaluation of the financial condition and earning power of a person rather than a business.

Most firms produce regular yearly statements, and in many cases, interim (usually quarterly) statements. The statements are prepared by, or at least with the assistance of, professional accountants. This usually assures a professional level of competency, but it does not mean consistency in the way assets, liabilities, income or expenses are reported. There is a great deal of latitude within acceptable accounting methods.

AUDITED AND UNAUDITED STATEMENTS

The annual statements of virtually all large companies are audited by independent accounting firms, but most small companies prefer to avoid the expense of paying for an independent audit. Thus, most of the statements received by most commercial lending officers will not be audited.

The purpose of the audit is to give the company's management a professional, outside opinion as to the fairness and adequacy of the company's financial reporting. The opinions stated by the auditors are therefore of meaning to potential lenders, investors and others who must rely on the company's statements. The auditor will evaluate the accounting methods used by the company, and upon completion of its auditing tests, issue its opinion. The opinion usually takes one of four forms: unqualified, qualified, adverse or disclaimer.

Unqualified Opinion

The *unqualified opinion,* in addition to describing the "scope" of the audit, essentially says that the financial statements "present fairly" the financial position of the company. However, the opinion is not a guarantee. Company management, not the auditor, is responsible for the statements. The audit has shown that management has confidence in its financial reporting, and the unqualified opinion is justification for that confidence.

Other Opinions

A *qualified opinion* is issued when the auditing firm has some questions or uncertainty regarding one or more reporting methods. An *adverse opinion* is given when major exceptions are found in the reporting processes. A *disclaimer opinion* is given when the audit was so limited (or nonexistent) that no conclusions can be reached by the auditing firm. In each situation, the opinion will set forth the reasons why less than an unqualified opinion was issued.

The auditor's opinion and the knowledge that the auditor reviewed a company's reporting processes is valuable to a commercial lender. However, while the annual statements of large borrowers normally are audited, statements of smaller companies seldom are. These smaller borrowers comprise the greatest number of commercial borrowers. Thus, careful analysis of statements is vital. This analysis should include at least three years' statements to improve the chances of identifying inconsistencies, unexplained changes in accounting methods or other distortions.

FOOTNOTES TO STATEMENTS

Because financial statements can be prepared in several ways, footnotes to the statement are used to explain the accounting procedures followed. Evaluation of financial statements should not be undertaken without prior reading of the footnotes. Only three of the many possible items which footnotes could cover will be described here: calculation of depreciation, inventory evaluation and treatment of the investment tax credit.

Calculation of Depreciation

An example of straight-line depreciation was used earlier in this chapter. A building was presumed to have a 20-year life, and 1/20 of its cost was to be written off each year. The Internal Revenue Service sets minimum time periods over which the cost of fixed assets can be written off, but it sets no maximum. It also allows the use of accelerated depreciation methods. Only one method–double-declining balance–will be mentioned here for illustration purposes.

The computation of depreciation by the double-declining balance method first requires computation of the rate of depreciation under the straight-line method. If twenty years is the period used, 1/20 equals five percent. Next, that rate is doubled (ten percent) and applied each year to the undepreciated balance of the asset. In the case of the building, for the first four years depreciation would be computed as follows:

Year	Depreciation Calculation	Depreciation Expense	Remaining Book Value
1	10% of $100,000	$10,000	$90,000
2	10% of 90,000	9,000	81,000
3	10% of 81,000	8,100	72,900
4	10% of 72,900	7,290	65,610

Had Mr. Jones used the double-declining balance method he would have charged $10,000 to depreciation expense in his first year rather than $5,000. His net income would have been $2,500 less, but so would his taxes. However, his building would have been reported on his year-end balance sheet at a book value of $90,000 rather than $95,000.

The choice of depreciation methods can make a significant difference in the values reported on the financial statements. A footnote should clarify the method(s) used.

Inventory Valuation

Companies also are allowed a choice as to the method of costing inventory used during a period. The choice affects the cost figures shown on the income statement as well as the value of inventory shown on the balance sheet. The LIFO (last-in, first-out) method assumes that inventories sold during a period were the last purchased, while the FIFO (first-in, first-out) method assumes inventories sold during the period were the earliest purchased. When prices are rising, LIFO places a higher cost on goods sold than FIFO, and thus results in lower earnings and taxes. The value of inventory on the year-end balance sheet is less using LIFO because the lowest cost inventory is assumed to be that still on hand.

In periods of rising prices, the use of FIFO tends to overstate earnings and give the highest inventory value on the balance sheet. This makes the company appear to be performing well, but at the sacrifice of higher income taxes.

Investment Tax Credit

Many of the fixed assets which companies buy qualify for the investment tax credit. If, for example, a machine costs $100,000 and the investment tax credit is 10 percent, the company can take $10,000 off its federal income tax bill for that year. How that tax credit is treated can make a significant difference in the income reported by the company.

The company can "flow through" the $10,000 in the year in which the asset is purchased, that is, take the entire $10,000 off its current year's taxes and show a net income $10,000 higher than would have been shown had the asset not been purchased. Or the company can "amortize" the $10,000 over the life of the machine. Assume the machine is expected to have a five-year life. Under the amortization method, income taxes would be reduced and net income increased $2,000 each of those five years.

These two brief examples show that the treatment of the investment tax credit can have a significant impact on one-year's earnings. The commercial lending officer should look to the footnotes for an explanation of its treatment.

BASIC FINANCE CONCEPTS

The terms used in finance and more particularly in commercial lending should trigger specific meanings to those involved with business loans. If these basic concepts are mastered they can be of significant help in the commercial lending process. Those defined below are: cash flow, liquidity, leverage and the risks common to commercial lending. In addition, the matching principle and floating-rate debt instruments are defined.

CASH FLOW

In the financial world, one word or term often has two or more meanings. These meanings may be related, but unless the person using the term is clear as to which meaning he or she wants to apply, confusion can result. *Cash flow* is a term that can lead to confusion, but its understanding is vital to anyone involved in commercial lending.

Many times the person referring to cash flow is talking about the funds flows within the firm shown by the sources and uses statement. A related, and more often used, meaning of cash flow is "the firm's ability to generate cash." It is even called cash throw-off by some practitioners. In this sense, *cash flow* for a period is the total of net income after taxes plus noncash expenses. Conceptually, it is a measure of the firm's ability to produce cash without any changes in liabilities or assets except for the depreciation charge.

It is easy to see that net income is a source of usable dollars, but giving the same status to noncash expenses (depreciation in the example of the Jones Store) may require some thought. Once again, the income statement for the Jones Store should be examined. Had there been no depreciation charge of $5,000, net income would have been $2,500 more, but so would income taxes. Had there been no depreciation charge, cash flow would have been the $10,000 of net income. With the depreciation charge, cash flow is $12,500 ($7,500 net income plus $5,000 depreciation). Cash flow is $2,500 more than it would have been had there been no depreciation charge, and that $2,500 is the amount of taxes saved. Cash flow is important to commercial lenders as they estimate the future debt repayment ability of borrowers.

LIQUIDITY

Another concept of importance is liquidity. In the most basic sense, *liquidity* is the quality of an asset which is its "closeness to cash." The most liquid asset is cash. If an asset is quite liquid it can be converted to cash rapidly with very little if any sacrifice of value. A Treasury bill is liquid because there is a very wide and active market for T bills, their quality is the highest and they are of very short maturity. They can be sold in a short time (virtually in minutes) no matter what is happening to the economy.

At the other end of the spectrum, a commercial building designed specifically to meet the requirements of a particular manufacturing process may require a very lengthy selling process and be sold at a sacrifice price if no buyer who needs its unique features can be found. All assets are liquid or illiquid by degrees, and their degree of liquidity at any point in time may depend on conditions in the economy. Most assets, particularly business assets, become less liquid as the economy enters a recessionary period.

The concept of liquidity can be expanded to include the collection of assets and liabilities comprising a firm's balance sheet. If, at an unlikely extreme, a firm were financed entirely by owner's equity and its assets consisted entirely of Treasury bills, then the firm would be extremely liquid. If instead, the assets were cases of canned fruits and vegetables from the current year's crop, it would still be quite liquid, though less so. And, the firm would be even less liquid if the assets consisted entirely of machines and buildings designed to produce a particular product for which there was no longer any demand.

Liquidity of the firm is a function of its liabilities, as well as its assets. In all three of the examples given above, the firm would be less liquid if there were debt in its balance sheet as well as owner's equity. The greater the proportion of the right side of the balance sheet comprised of debt, the less liquid the firm. In other words, the greater the financial leverage used by the firm, the less the liquidity. And, if a large portion of the debt is current liabilities, the firm is less liquid than if the debt is long term. A firm is said to be illiquid when it does not have enough funds to meet its obligations, which could be the case if it had a large amount of current liabilities financing long-term assets which could be sold only at great sacrifice of value.

Matching Principle

This rule of thumb is intended as a guide to help avoid the problems of illiquidity. It holds that the firm should finance short-term uses with short-term sources and long-term uses with long-term sources. This concept will be extended in Chapter 5.

Profitability Versus Liquidity

A profitable firm is not automatically liquid. In fact, many firms which are increasing profits every year are becoming less liquid every year. Commercial loan officers must be aware that this could happen to borrowing customers. How does it happen? An illustration can be drawn using the case of Mr. Jones' business. Assume that after producing a profit of $7,500 his first year, he decides to make a $50,000 addition to his building. If he increased his mortgage by $50,000 to pay for the addition then his business is somewhat less liquid. He now has additional interest and principal payments to make. If instead he generated the $50,000 by allowing trade credit (accounts payable) to expand, then his firm would be much less liquid. In effect, a long-term asset is being financed by a short-term source. Any decline in business could create serious problems for Mr. Jones.

Examples similar to Mr. Jones' situation are not unusual, and a lender can suddenly find its loans difficult to collect. A profitable firm can also lose liquidity due to mistakes in acquiring inventory that does not sell or by extending credit to customers who do not pay. Such mistakes sooner or later result in reduced profitability, but this usually is not reflected in the income statement until long after the mistakes are made.

RISK CLASSIFICATIONS

Recognizing risk means that one is aware that disappointing results may take place in the future. Financial people identify three classes of risk which pertain to commercial lending. *Credit risk* refers to the possibility that a borrower will experience disappointing business results that will impair the ability to meet scheduled loan payments. The *interest rate risk* pertains to the possibility that interest rates will rise and reduce the values of outstanding, fixed-rate debt instruments such as bonds and mortgages. The negative effect of rising interest rates is described later in the chapter. *Financial risk* results from the use of debt, that is, creating financial leverage.

FINANCIAL LEVERAGE

When financial people use the term *leverage*, they are referring to the use of debt by the firm. This is more precisely called financial leverage. Another form of leverage, operating leverage, will be described in Chapter 5.

The concept of financial leverage can be grasped by thinking of debt as a tool used by the firm to try to lever upwards the return on the owner's equity. For example, if a debt-free firm with $100,000 owner's equity earned $20,000, then its rate of return on owner's equity for the year would be:

$$\frac{20,000}{100,000} = 20\%$$

If management decides at the beginning of the next year to borrow $100,000 at 10 percent, the firm would now have $200,000 at work. If it is again able to earn 20 percent (before interest charges and ignoring tax), then for the second year its rate of return on owner's equity is:

$$\frac{\$40,000 - \$10,000\ \text{interest}}{\$100,000} = 30\%$$

The use of debt has levered upwards its rate of return to owner's equity from 20 to 30 percent. This result is referred to as positive leverage. But leverage can also be negative. Assume the second year results were not as good as the first year's, and the rate of return on total investment was only five percent or $10,000. Then the rate of return on owner's equity would have been:

$$\frac{\$10,000 - \$10,000\ \text{interest}}{\$100,000} = 0\%$$

Negative leverage has resulted, levering downwards the rate from five to zero percent. Obviously, if results had been any poorer, the use of leverage would have resulted in a loss. Thus, the use of financial leverage can be beneficial or damaging, depending on the success of the firm's operations.

NEGATIVE EFFECT OF RISING INTEREST RATES

When interest rates rise, the values of outstanding debt instruments decline. Also, the longer the maturity date of a given debt instrument the more it will decline in value with a given rise in interest rates. In the financial world, this is called the "interest rate risk."

The reason outstanding debt instruments lose value when interest rates rise is because an investor can buy newly created debt instruments paying the new, higher rates, and so will not pay face value for an older debt instrument that was originated at a much lower rate. To sell the older instrument, the holder must discount it. And the more distant the maturity, the more it must be discounted after a specific rise in interest rates.

The interest rate risk can be illustrated by referring back to Figure 1-5. All of the bonds listed in the figure were sold originally to investors at, or very close to, face value. By looking at the yield column, it can be seen that a new bond, if issued on the date of the list (July 31, 1980), would have had an interest rate in the area of 10 to 11 percent. The issues on the list with original interest rates below that level had prices (see the bid column) well below face value.

Two issues on the list with 7 7/8 percent rates point up the impact of the interest rate risk. One has a maturity date of February 15, 1993, and the second matures February 15, 2000. The first had a bid price of 80.20 (80 and 20/32), or $806.25 per $1,000 bond, and the second had a bid price of 76.16 (76 and 16/32) or $765 per $1,000 bond. Thus, the effect of rising interest rates was to depress the values of both issues, and the longer-term issue was impacted most because its more distant maturity required a greater discount to make it yield a market rate of return.

FLOATING RATE INSTRUMENTS

Because of the negative effect of the rising interest rates of the 1960s and 1970s, more and more debt instruments are issued today at floating rather than fixed rates. For example, bonds are issued by corporations on which the interest rate is adjusted every six months according to changes in the yields on six-month Treasury bills. The purpose of the rate adjustment is to prevent sharp declines in the market value of the bonds if interest rates rise.

Commercial lenders rely heavily on floating rates on all but the shortest-term loans. By 1978, over half of the loans made by commercial banks were on a floating rate basis. This has been an important factor in keeping commercial bank revenues increasing as interest rates rose sharply in 1979, 1980 and 1981.

BASIC INTEREST RATE CONCEPTS

Interest rates have been discussed in numerous contexts up to this point in the text. Brief consideration of the basic elements of interest rates is appropriate here.

GENERAL INTEREST EQUATION

Interest is the payment for the use of an amount of money for a period of time. The general equation for calculating interest is:

$$I = P \times R \times T$$

Where: I = the dollar amount of interest
P = principal, the amount borrowed
R = the interest rate
T = the period of time

So that if $200 is borrowed for one year at the annual rate of 12 percent, then

$$I = \$200 \times .12 \times 1 = \$24$$

COMPOUND INTEREST

When interest earned during one period is not paid but is added to the principal, it becomes part of the principal and earns interest in the second period. Suppose the above loan was to be paid at the end of two years, including all interest earned. Then at the start of the second year principal would be $224, and

$$I = \$224 \times .12 \times 1 = \$26.88$$

Interest earned the second year was $26.88. There was "interest on interest" of $2.88. The total due at the end of two years is $250.88. The formula for compound interest is:

$$I = P(1+I)^T - P$$

In the above example:

$$I = \$200(1.12)^2 - 200$$
$$= \$200(1.2544) - 200 = \$50.88$$

Rule of 72

A handy rule of thumb which is often of help in making interest rate decisions is the Rule of 72. If the number 72 is divided by a given rate, the result is the number of years required, with annual compounding, for a given amount to double. For example, if $100 is invested at eight percent, compounded annually, in nine years it will be worth approximately $200.

The rule works for declining values as well. How long does it take for a dollar to lose half its purchasing power at an inflation rate of twelve percent? If twelve is divided into 72, the answer produced is six years.

Rule of 78s

This rule concerns the computation of the balance remaining when an installment loan is paid before due. It has the effect of loading a major portion of the contract interest in the early installments. The latter payments apply largely to principal.

Under this rule, a sum is computed using the number of payments in the contract. If monthly payments are required for a year, then $12+11+10+9+8+7+6+5+4+3+2+1 = 78$. When the first payment is received, 12/78 of the total interest due is assumed to be paid, with the balance of the payment going to reduce principal. The second payment is deemed to include 11/78 of interest due and so on.

DISCOUNT BASIS

The interest on some financial instruments, including some commercial loans, is computed on a discount basis. For example, a loan might be for one year, the amount to be paid at that time is $100, and the lender stated a discount of eight percent. The borrower received $92, and one year later paid $100. Was the true rate eight percent?

These amounts can be substituted into the general interest equation to show the difference between discount and simple interest and find the true rate.

$$\$8 = 92 \times R \times 1$$
$$R = 8/92 = 8.7\%$$

When a rate is stated on a discount basis, the true or simple rate is higher.

SUMMARY

A good understanding of business financial statements and various basic financial concepts is essential knowledge for anyone involved in commercial lending. The balance sheet, income statement, and sources and uses statement are fundamental reports prepared by businesses. Although there are significant differences from company to company in the methods of preparation and manner of presentation of statements, consistent accounting principles underlie all financial statements. The commercial loan officer should be familiar with these principles.

Several financial concepts are integral to the commercial lending process. Cash flow refers to the firm's ability to generate cash from operations. It consists of net income plus noncash expenditures, chiefly depreciation.

Liquidity is a quality of an asset that describes how easily and at what risk of loss, it can be converted to cash. This quality can be imputed to a balance sheet and includes not only the liquidity of the firm's assets, but its liabilities (their extent and makeup) as well. A profitable firm does not necessarily have liquidity and vice versa.

Financial leverage refers to the "leveraging" effect on income from the use of debt. Use of financial leverage creates financial risk.

The interest rate risk refers to the potential loss in the value of fixed-rate instruments when interest rates rise as well as to the reduced rate of earnings experienced when a lender is locked into previously made, low-yield debt instruments. Floating rate instruments have been a response to the sharply higher interest rates of recent years.

Basic interest rate concepts include the general interest equation, compound interest and the discount basis of computing interest. Two rules of finance are the Rule of 72 and the Rule of 78s.

CHAPTER QUESTIONS

1. Why does a balance sheet balance?

2. What is depreciation in the accounting sense?   Accelerated depreciation?

3. In a sources and uses statement, is an increase in a liability a source or a use? An increase in an asset?

4. What is meant if the auditor's opinion on a set of financial statements is unqualified?

5. What is the purpose of financial statement footnotes?

6. Give an example of an asset which is very liquid. One which is very illiquid.

7. What is the risk that results when a firm uses financial leverage?

8. What is the rule of 72? The rule of 78s?

3

Short-Term Commercial Loans

OBJECTIVES

After reading Chapter 3, you should be able to:

- Describe seasonal lending to business;
- Define "self-liquidating";
- Explain lines of credit;
- Explain compensating balances;
- Discuss why some commercial loans are secured and others unsecured;
- Explain asset-based financing;
- Describe five ways in which short-term loans are secured;
- Illustrate the use of letters of credit.

This chapter discusses several forms of commercial loans that are classified as short-term. Although the designation short-term implies that a given borrower pays off an obligation within a matter of months, this is not necessarily the result. Loans are classified as short-term because they finance short-term uses, and they are due in less than one year. In many cases, institutions make these loans on a demand basis. That means the lender has the right to call in the loan at any time. Chapter 4 describes loans made for longer-term uses with specified maturities beyond one year.

SEASONAL LOANS

Those business loans that normally are paid off in less than one year and are required to finance some recurring but temporary expansion are *seasonal loans*. An example of a seasonal loan follows. It is based on a hypothetical neighborhood drug store.

FINANCING A CHRISTMAS INVENTORY

The neighborhood drug store conducts a stable business throughout most of the year, but sales increase sharply during the Christmas season because the owner, Mr. Smith, stocks several lines of merchandise suitable for Christmas giving. He buys the merchandise from several wholesalers and pays them when the goods are delivered to his store.

Mr. Smith does not have enough capital to pay for the goods, so he borrows what he needs. The term of the loan is only a few weeks, until it can reasonably be expected that the merchandise will be sold. The amount of the loan probably is somewhat less than the total amount needed to pay the suppliers. For this example, it can be assumed the goods cost $50,000 and the amount of the loan is $40,000. The lender is provided a comfort margin because Mr. Smith has $10,000 of his own invested in the inventory.

If Christmas sales are good, Mr. Smith will be able to repay the $40,000 loan plus interest, recover his $10,000 and still make a profit. He will have had additional expenses as a result of the increased sales volume, perhaps for temporary clerical help, but if his mark-up is adequate, he will make a profit, the financial intermediary will be repaid with interest, and both will be satisfied.

Self-liquidating Feature

The loan to Mr. Smith was "self-liquidating," a feature of many short-term loans. *Self-liquidating* means that the asset financed is sold, producing the cash to pay off the loan. Until the early twentieth century, most of the commercial loans made by commercial banks were short-term, self-liquidating loans. This seemed much safer than lending to finance equipment, manufacturing facilities or other assets not intended for direct conversion to cash. However, a rapidly expanding economy in early twentieth century America required extensive amounts of longer-term capital, so commercial banks gradually began providing a portion of that capital.

When the loan to Mr. Smith is considered, it is clear that the self-liquidating feature was more important to the lender than whether or not Mr. Smith made a profit on the merchandise. Had the Christmas sales been disappointing and Mr. Smith received only $45,000 for the goods (which cost him $50,000), he would have lost part of the $10,000 he invested in the goods, but there would have been sufficient funds for the lender to be repaid. Of course, the lender would have preferred that Mr. Smith make a profit, and the fact that he lost money may discourage the lender from advancing as much next year. It will be pointed out in future chapters that liquidity (see Chapter 2) in the balance sheet is more important in short-term lending than profitability of the firm. A self-liquidating asset obviously is liquid.

OTHER SEASONAL LOANS

In addition to financing temporary increases in retail inventories, seasonal loans are used in many areas of business, including manufacturing and farming.

Manufacturing Loans

Manufacturing firms use seasonal loans to build up inventories of finished goods in anticipation of future sales. The seasonal loan is used to purchase raw materials, pay employees and meet other expenses while the products are being manufactured. As the inventory of finished goods is sold, the loan is repaid. In many cases the manufacturing firm sells on terms, that is the buyer is allowed a period of perhaps 30 or 60 days to pay the manufacturer. During this period the manufacturer has accounts receivable. When the receivables are paid, the manufacturer can repay the seasonal loan.

This process is called the *cash cycle.* Proceeds of the seasonal loan followed a course through the purchase of raw materials and payment of other expenses into the finished product. Upon sale of the finished product the funds were embodied in accounts receivable. When these were collected and the loan repaid the cash cycle was completed.

Examples of products often produced on a seasonal basis are bicycles, snowmobiles, swimwear, school books, lawn and garden equipment, and those items associated with Christmas, Easter or Valentine's Day. Processing of fruits and vegetables is, of course, seasonal and requires a large investment of funds as inventories of the processed items build up. Some products that are sold on a seasonal basis are produced at a level rate if they are not subject to spoilage or obsolescence and if the manufacturer has the financial strength to keep funds tied up in inventory for lengthy periods.

Farming Loans

Farmers borrow large amounts on a seasonal basis in order to plant, raise and harvest crops. Expenses for seed, fertilizer, insect control, labor and operating expenses must be paid long before payment for the crop is received. Seasonal loans to farmers include the same considerations as those made to other types of businesses. Farming carries some risks; the most obvious of which is adverse weather.

A freeze in Florida may destroy a citrus crop and as a result a farmer may experience a losing season. The loss is not due to an error in forecasting business conditions, a failure to judge the market for the produce or any of the other reasons many businesses experience losses. Financial intermediaries making seasonal loans to farmers recognize the additional risk imposed by possible adverse weather conditions and plan ahead for the possibility that all or a part of a loan may be carried over to the next season. Loan carry-overs are common in farm lending.

Another risk common to farming may be termed price risk. A good crop year may result in sharp price declines. Farmers who have done an excellent job of producing a crop may actually experience losses because overall crop production was outstanding. Some farmers may sell only a portion of their crop at the depressed prices, storing a portion for later sale. In such cases, they may need additional credit to carry the stored crops.

LINES OF CREDIT

Temporary financing, including seasonal lending, is often carried out through a *line of credit*. This is an arrangement whereby the potential borrower plans well ahead of time how much short-term credit will be needed and asks the financial intermediary if it will stand ready to advance those funds when needed.

MR. SMITH'S LINE OF CREDIT

Mr. Smith might have arranged a line of credit as he was planning the purchase of Christmas merchandise. The line of credit allows Mr. Smith to order merchandise well ahead of the Christmas rush and set the desired delivery dates knowing he will have funds to make payment when the goods arrive.

He would have met with his loan officer, and, based on Smith's strong financial condition and past record of profitable Christmas seasons, the loan officer will indicate that the loan proceeds will be advanced as Mr. Smith needs them. The indication may be verbal or the loan officer may give Mr. Smith a letter stating the amount of the line, the period during which the line can be drawn down and when repayment is expected. Mr. Smith may be required to sign a note for the full amount of the line at the time the agreement is reached. Or, as he draws amounts under the line of credit, he may sign notes each time for the amount drawn.

A line of credit normally is not considered to be legally binding. It is an informal indication of willingness to lend up to a certain amount. In some cases, courts have held that a line of credit agreement does constitute a formal agreement and thus is binding to the lender. Sometimes the line of credit is in the form of a definite commitment whereby the agreement is formal and a commitment fee is charged by the lender. If Mr. Smith's business suddenly declined sharply, or the financial intermediary itself encountered serious problems, then it might not comply with the line of credit. Short of some clear-cut justification, however, it would be very poor business for the financial institution to not comply with the agreement.

USING THE LINE OF CREDIT

The line of credit works well, not only for temporary expansion of retail inventories such as Mr. Smith's, but also for seasonal manufacturing processes and agricultural loans. It is an excellent part of a business' planning process to set up the line well in advance of need; lenders encourage that this be done. A line of credit also helps the financial institution in its planning process, because it can prepare to have funds ready when it is expected that the line will be drawn down.

Drawing Down and Repaying the Line

A line of credit frequently is drawn down in pieces and may be repaid the same way. For example, a swimwear manufacturer may begin producing swimsuits in November for placement on store shelves the following spring. As the production process goes forward and inventory builds up, the line is gradually drawn down. Then, during the late winter and early spring, the manufacturer gradually sells the swimwear, converting it to accounts receivable and in turn, to cash. As cash is received the line is gradually paid off, a process that may take several months. Then, after two or three months of being out of debt, the process begins again.

Interest Rate on the Line

When the line of credit is originated the method of charging interest is determined. Since interest rates, and particularly short-term rates, are so volatile (see Chapter 1), commercial banks usually charge a floating rate tied to the prime rate. For example, the rate might be set at two percentage points above the bank's prime rate. In some cases, the rate may be set at a percentage of the bank's prime rate, such as 115 percent of prime. Thus, if the prime was ten percent, the rate on the amount of the line being used would be 11-1/2 percent.[1]

COMPENSATING BALANCES

Commercial banks, on occasion, have required compensating balances in connection with lines of credit. The business firm receiving the line of credit is expected to maintain a certain balance in its checking account at the bank. These idle balances, in turn, are used by the bank for loans and investments, thus effectively increasing its return over the interest rate charged when the line is drawn down.

A common way in which compensating balance requirements are applied is to require that the business firm keep an amount, say 10 percent of the line, on deposit before any funds are drawn. As funds are drawn, additional balances of, say 10 percent of the amount drawn must be maintained. For example, if the line was for $60,000, the firm must maintain a deposit of $6,000 until funds are drawn. If the first draw is $20,000, then the compensating balance would increase to $8,000. When the entire line was drawn, the balance required would be $12,000. The effect, of course, is to increase the cost of the line to the business, because it could use the funds elsewhere or borrow $12,000 less under the line of credit if there were no compensating balance requirement.

Banks seem to be gradually replacing the compensating balance

---

[1] Randall C. Merris, "Business Loans at Large Commercial Banks: Policies and Practices," *Economic Perspectives*, November/December 1979, pp. 15-23.

requirement with commitment fees for agreeing to the line and higher rates of interest on amounts drawn down. The extent of this practice, though, may depend on the competitive environment at the time the line of credit is granted. The commitment fee may be, for example, one-half of one percent of the line and is payment to the bank for standing ready to advance funds.

BACKUP LINES

Many large, creditworthy corporations borrow short-term funds by issuing commercial paper (see Chapter 1). Lenders who place their funds in commercial paper do not have specific collateral, that is, the issuance of commercial paper is a form of unsecured borrowing. Therefore, the lenders want some assurance that the corporate borrowers have access to enough cash to pay off the commercial paper at maturity. This assurance is provided by lines of credit which the corporations have arranged with commercial banks. They are commonly termed commercial paper backup lines and are restricted to that use. These lines are seldom if ever used. They serve an insurance function rather than providing large amounts of funds to the corporation. The lines usually are paid for with compensating balances.

SECURED OR UNSECURED

Many loans to businesses are made with no specific pledge of collateral required by the lender. That means the loans are *unsecured*. Financially strong companies with proven business histories that borrow amounts that are small relative to their net worth are more likely to receive loans on an unsecured basis. Because of their financial strength and the smaller workload of the lender (less documentation, no collateral control), such companies usually pay lower interest rates for unsecured credit than other companies pay for borrowing on a secured basis.

Short-term, self-liquidating loans are more likely to be made unsecured than are intermediate-term loans, particularly if the merchandise financed is of recognized quality. Outcomes are much more predictable in the period covered by a short-term loan than in a period covering several years. Also, the cash cycle of loan proceeds to inventory to accounts receivable to cash is much more predictable than, say, the benefits to be derived over several years from the purchase of a new piece of manufacturing equipment.

Mr. Smith might borrow on an unsecured basis if he has a good loan repayment record, strong financial condition and a history of successful Christmas selling. The lender will require financial statements periodically, showing personal assets and liabilities as well as those of the store. However, if Mr. Smith does not totally qualify for unsecured credit, the lender should require collateral. The simplicity of lending without security should not be allowed to lure the lender into not requiring collateral.

Also, a lender should not look to collateral to justify making a loan that should not be made. The purpose in taking collateral is to increase the assurance the loan will be repaid. No lender wants to look to collateral for debt repayment, it is simply a final resort.

ASSET-BASED FINANCING

The preference of commercial lenders long has been to make short-term, self-liquidating loans to financially strong companies on an unsecured basis. Such loans were safe and not complicated by the need to control collateral. Over the past 12 to 15 years, the growing need for all forms of capital on the part of business and the increased need for profits on the part of financial intermediaries has brought a large increase in secured commercial lending. The general term for secured commercial lending is *asset-based financing*.

To be competitive in commercial lending, a financial intermediary cannot avoid asset-based financing. However, the emphasis on collateral should not be overdone. To many, the concept of asset-based financing suggests that as long as the borrower has unpledged assets of value, credit can be extended. While understanding the nature of business assets, how to assess their value and maintain control is vital to asset-based financing, loans must still be based on the overall liquidity, financial condition and profit potential of the firm.[2]

METHODS OF SECURING SHORT-TERM CREDIT

Where collateral is required to secure short-term credit, the asset financed usually serves as collateral. In some cases additional collateral is required. And in other cases, the loan purpose is not to finance the

[2] Keith L. Stock, "Asset-Based Financing: Borrower and Lender Perspectives," *The Journal of Commercial Bank Lending*, December 1980, pp. 31-46.

asset that serves as collateral, although on the surface it may appear as such. For example, a firm may want to borrow against its accounts receivable because last year it used all its liquidity in the construction of a special purpose building. The sources and uses of funds statement (discussed in Chapter 2) shows how funds flow constantly between assets and liabilities. That continuous funds flow should be kept in mind by the lender as the potential borrower describes the loan purpose. This section will stress methods of securing short-term credit rather than loan purpose, though in some cases purpose is obvious.

Uniform Commercial Code

Until the 1950s each state had its own unique regulations governing commercial transactions, including secured lending. The design of the *Uniform Commercial Code*, which was intended to unify all of the law pertaining to commercial transactions, was initially undertaken in 1944 by the National Conference of Commissions on Uniform State Laws and the American Law Institute. It was first adopted in Pennsylvania in 1953 and is now in effect in all 50 states. Each state has made some revisions in the Code, so complete uniformity does not exist. Article 9 of the Code is concerned with secured loans.

The lender accepting collateral for a loan seeks to establish a "security interest" in the loan. The security interest is the lender's rights in the property allowing the lender to assert legal claim in the case of default. The lender's rights precede those of the borrower, other creditors and any third parties. When this happens, the lender's security interest is said to be "perfected."

Security Agreements

The contract between the borrower and lender wherein the borrower assigns the collateral to the lender is the *security agreement*. The exact form of the security agreement varies from state to state, and it may be general in form or pertain only to specific types of collateral such as inventory or accounts receivable. In all cases it defines the collateral and sets forth numerous warranties and covenants on the part of the borrower. One of these will be that the borrower will keep the collateral insured. Another could be that the borrower continue in its present place of business.

Floating Liens

The financial intermediary that provided the loan to Mr. Smith might have deemed that the loan could be made only on a secured basis, using his inventory as collateral. The lender would have had Mr. Smith sign a security agreement. The security agreement established the lender's security interest in Mr. Smith's inventory, but the lender's claim was not limited to the Christmas merchandise. The floating lien concept, which derives from the Uniform Commercial Code, means that a security agreement may provide that collateral, whenever acquired, will secure all obligations covered by the agreement. The floating lien, established by the security agreement, gives the lender recourse to Mr. Smith's entire inventory without the requirement that specific items be identified as those financed.

The limited control over inventory provided the lender by the floating lien must be recognized. This point will be obvious as other forms of securing loans with inventory are examined below. If the borrower is not considered an adequate risk to borrow on an unsecured basis, then the floating lien is of only modest value in reducing that risk.

Floor-plan Lending

Many retail products, such as autos, boats and television sets, are large, individualistic and expensive. Such items are frequently financed for retailers through a method called *floor planning*. This method allows the retailer to display the items while they remain under the control of the lender. The lender retains title to the merchandise until it is sold. This is accomplished through the use of a "trust receipt."

The name, serial number and other information about the inventory items are recorded on the trust receipt. The trust receipt shows the lender to be legal owner. In the case of automobiles and other items that have recordable titles, the titles would also be held by the lender. When an item is sold, a sufficient amount of the proceeds is delivered to the lender to retire the debt against that item, and title is transferred to the buyer. The lender may provide financing to the buyer, in some cases, as a result of its close relationship with the retailer.

From time to time the lender will conduct flooring inspections to make sure none of the items has been "sold out of trust." A flooring inspection is an unannounced visit by a representative of the lender to the retailer's place of business. The serial numbers of each item are matched against the serial numbers on the trust receipts held by the lender. Should it be found that an item has been sold out of trust, the proceeds can be claimed by the lender because they are considered to be held in trust by the retailer for the lender, just as was the inventory item.

Loans on Warehouse Receipts

Many forms of inventory, such as canned goods, grain, lumber and raw materials used in manufacturing, may serve as collateral if they are placed under control of a third party who guarantees their availability in case the lender must take possession. This function is performed by a bonded public warehouse. The goods may be delivered to a warehouse by the borrower. The warehouse company would then issue receipts for the goods which the lender would hold as collateral.

The warehouse company will release the goods only upon return of the receipts. The borrower cannot take possession without paying the lender or arranging the substitution of other collateral.[3]

Some inventory items could be delivered to a warehouse only with great difficulty. For example, a pile of logs at a sawmill is very valuable, but very difficult to move to a warehouse. In such a case, a warehouse company may establish a "field warehouse" at the sawmill. The logs, which serve as collateral, are placed under control of the warehouse company, segregated sufficiently so they can be separately identified and warehouse receipts are issued.

Pledging Accounts Receivable

Many firms extend credit to their customers in order to generate a higher level of sales than would be possible if sales were on a cash only basis. If the customers of such firms are good credit risks, then the accounts receivable resulting from credit sales are high quality assets and may serve as collateral. Some firms become too aggressive in trying to increase sales by extending credit, and consequently the receivables they hold may be largely those of financially weak creditors.

Normally the amount loaned against receivables is well below their face value, perhaps only 50 or 60 percent. More may be provided if the company and its customers have good payment records.

Usually, with accounts receivable loans, the customer is not informed that the receivable has been pledged. The borrowing firm continues to collect the receivables, but then remits funds to the lender identifying the receivables to which the payments apply. If the loan is made on a notification basis, the borrowing firm's customers are advised or notified that their obligations are pledged and that they are to make payment to the lender.

Notification implies that the lender does not trust the borrowing firm to remit payments as collected. If notification is the only way the lender will consider making an accounts receivable loan, then it is questionable whether the loan should be made at all. Borrowing firms obviously prefer nonnotification so that their customers are not aware that they are pledging the receivables.

Factoring

In some industries, notably furniture and textile manufacturing, it is more common to sell receivables outright rather than borrow against them. This activity, called factoring, represents sale of assets rather

---

[3] Readers may be interested in reading *The Great Salad Oil Swindle* by Norman C. Miller (New York, NY: Coward, McCann, 1965) as an example of the risks involved in lending on warehouse receipts (and secured lending in general).

than borrowing, but its net effect is little different for the borrower from pledging receivables.

Factoring is the principal activity for a few finance companies, but only one of many for other financial intermediaries. Receivables are purchased at a discount from face value. The discount, or commission, may be one or two percent. The purchase is normally on a nonrecourse basis, and a portion of the amount due the seller is withheld in case of nonpayment of some receivables. The factor may also provide credit analysis for the selling firm, collection service and bookkeeping, thus relieving the seller from the need of operating a credit department.

Other Short-term Lending Arrangements

Besides the methods of securing short-term credit described above, others include: real property as security for construction loans, pledging of stocks and bonds, assigning the cash value of life insurance, guarantees of other parties and assignment of contracts.[4]

Construction Loans. When a business firm decides to construct a new building and if mortgage financing will be required, an early step is to obtain a commitment from a long-term lender for the mortgage loan. Since mortgage loan proceeds will not be advanced until the satisfactory completion of the building, a construction loan frequently is required.

The lender of the construction funds does not advance the entire loan at the outset. As portions of the work are completed, if specifications set by the long-term lender are being met, equivalent portions of the loan are advanced. Security for the construction loan is the property. When the building is completed to the satisfaction of the long-term lender, the lender pays off the construction loan and becomes the mortgagee.

Pledging Stocks and Bonds. Stocks and bonds owned by a company or separately by the company's owners may serve as collateral for short-term loans. Care should be taken to assure, as nearly as possible, that repayment of the loan will come from the operation of the business, and not from sale of the collateral.

For example, if the loan proceeds are for the purpose of seasonal expansion of inventory, then it is appropriate to expect repayment as the seasonal expansion is reversed and inventory turns back into cash. However, if the loan proceeds are used to remodel a store building,

---

[4] Of course, there is no limit on the number or type of borrowing arrangements secured by forms of property or future income streams. Virtually all forms of real and personal property are used to secure short-term commercial loans, as well as assignment of rights to future income. These may include, for example, royalty income and oil production. Obviously, the person involved in secured commercial lending must spend a significant amount of time in developing his or her understanding of all forms of collateral.

then generation of enough extra cash to repay the short-term loan could be impossible. The lender is faced with the alternative of renewing the short-term loan or forcing sale of the collateral. In the first case, the borrower has virtually forced the lender to provide longer-term financing against the lender's wishes. In the second case, a forced sale of the securities may create ill will for the lender, resulting in the borrower receiving a depressed price for the securities or otherwise cause disappointments.

Borrowing Against Life Insurance. The same considerations apply when the cash value of a life insurance policy is used as collateral as when securities are used. The loan must rest on its own merits as a short-term loan. The liquidity and ease of handling collateral should not be determining factors in deciding whether the loan should be made.

In making a life insurance loan, the policy must be assigned to the lender. A copy of the assignment is provided to the insurance company and the insurance company in turn must acknowledge receipt of the assignment.

Loan Guarantees. The borrower who does not have sufficient collateral may obtain the guaranty of a third party. In the case of a corporate borrower, the third party may be principal shareholders. It may be a supplier who wants to sell goods to the borrower but who does not want to incur debt by extending trade credit. Or, it could be an individual. In any case, the guarantee serves the same function as collateral and should not be the sole basis for making the loan. The guarantor should be a factor in influencing payment by the borrower, because the guarantor does not want to be called on to make repayment. Obviously, the guarantor should be apprised of the risk accompanying the supplying of a loan guarantee.

Assigned Contracts. Any business firm that receives a contract to provide products or services may need to borrow sufficient funds to fulfill the contract provisions. The assigned contract may serve as collateral for the loan. As payments are made under the contract they are delivered to the lender and used to reduce the loan.

The quality of the contract depends on two important considerations: the ability of the borrowing firm to perform under the terms of the contract and the ability of the other parties to the contract to make payments when due. Both of these considerations may be very complex to evaluate. As with all secured commercial loans, the lender must look beyond the collateral and examine carefully the overall financial strength and performance record of the borrower.

LETTERS OF CREDIT

A *letter of credit* is a contract between the seller and the financial intermediary. It sets forth the specific transactions covered, the amounts of the transactions and the date of expiration of the letter.

Letters of credit take several forms, the most common being the commercial letter of credit. It provides assurance to a seller of goods that payment will be received for the goods. The buyer of the goods arranges for the financial intermediary to issue the letter of credit for the benefit of the seller of the goods. As goods are delivered to the buyer, the seller presents drafts to the financial intermediary and receives payment for the goods. The drafts must be accompanied by appropriate documents showing that delivery of the goods conformed to the terms of the letter of credit.

The letter of credit allows the seller to look to the financial intermediary for payment, substituting its financial position for that of the buyer. The buyer either makes immediate payment to the financial intermediary or becomes obligated in the form of a short-term loan when the goods are paid for by the intermediary.

SUMMARY

Many forms of short-term business credit are advanced by financial intermediaries in the U.S. Commercial loans are classified as short-term based on the nature of the assets financed and the repayment terms of the loan. The underlying notes are due in less than one year or on demand.

Seasonal loans are made to finance a temporary increase in inventories and accounts receivable which result from temporary periods of expanded production or sales. Seasonal loans are self-liquidating as are most short-term business loans; that is, the asset financed converts to cash, supplying funds for repayment of the debt.

Seasonal and other short-term loans are often made through a line of credit agreement. The line of credit is an informal indication by the lender that it will stand ready to advance a given amount of funds during a stipulated period. The lender may require that the borrower maintain a certain level of compensating balances on deposit, both before and after amounts have been drawn under the line.

Short-term business loans may be unsecured or secured. Unsecured loans are made only to financially strong borrowers and, thus, interest rates are usually lower than those on secured loans. Also, the amount of time involved in making and supervising unsecured loans is less. Financial intermediaries generally favor unsecured lending. However, the financial intermediaries' need for profits and the capital needs of business have brought about a large increase in secured lending since the 1960s.

Secured lending, or asset-based financing, leans heavily on evaluation and control of the underlying collateral. Of at least equal importance, however, is proper financial analysis of the borrower.

Many approaches are followed in securing short-term business loans. These are regulated under Article 9 of the Uniform Commercial Code which has been adopted, with some variations, by all 50 states. The lender's rights in the collateral are called the security interest, and the contract establishing the security interest is the security agreement.

Inventories may serve as collateral by establishment of a floating lien (which gives the lender recourse to all the borrower's inventories, whenever acquired), through floor plan arrangements (whereby the lender holds legal title to the collateralized merchandise and releases title when proceeds of sale of the merchandise are remitted) and through warehousing arrangements (a warehouse company controls the inventory and its receipts serve as the basis of credit).

Accounts receivable may be pledged as collateral for short-term credit. Normally the borrower continues to collect the receivables and remits the funds to the lender. An arrangement whereby a financial intermediary purchases the receivables is called factoring.

Other short-term lending includes construction loans and loans secured by stocks and bonds, the cash value of life insurance, guaranties of third parties and assignment of contracts. Some short-term lending is preceded by a letter of credit, whereby the financial intermediary agrees to pay the seller of goods on delivery to the intermediary's customer.

CHAPTER QUESTIONS

1. What is a self-liquidating loan?
2. Describe the process of establishing, using and repaying a line of credit.
3. How does a floating lien function?
4. Give an example of a floor plan lending arrangement and explain how it would operate.
5. What is the purpose of a field warehouse?
6. What is a letter of credit? Give an example of its use.

4

Intermediate-Term Commercial Loans

OBJECTIVES

After reading Chapter 4, you should be able to:

- Explain the working capital concept;
- Illustrate what is meant by permanent current assets;
- Describe the purposes for which intermediate-term credit is extended;
- Differentiate revolving credit agreements from lines of credit;
- Define term lending;
- Explain why leasing is a form of intermediate financing;
- Summarize the important features of the Small Business Administration lending program;
- Explain the reason for emphasis on cash flow in intermediate-term lending.

This chapter discusses forms of intermediate-term business financing and develops some of the important concepts which should be understood by anyone involved in commercial lending. Unlike the loans described in Chapter 3 which were based on notes payable on demand or within a few months (even though many borrowers remain in debt for several years by frequently renewing short-term lending arrangements), the loans made under intermediate-term forms of credit have stated maturities extending more than one year. Few loans have maturities beyond seven years, though a loan maturing in up to ten years is made on occasion. In the world of finance, periods from one to ten years usually are considered intermediate-term. Long-term business credit usually takes the form of bonds sold in the capital market or mortgages on real property.

Intermediate-term loans are made for the purposes of acquiring fixed assets or for permanent additions to current assets. Since the idea of permanent additions to current assets sounds self-contradicting and because the underlying concept is important and often misunderstood, it will be explained before the types of intermediate credit are discussed.

CONCEPT OF WORKING CAPITAL

The term *working capital* is used frequently by accounting and finance people, but many of them do not have a clear, distinct concept for working capital that is of help to them in their work.[1] Some regard working capital as current assets. If this is the case, the term might as well be discarded. Why have another name for current assets?

Others define working capital as current assets minus current liabilities. This definition is sometimes called "net" working capital. It provides a method of measuring working capital, but having a method of measurement still does not provide a useful concept for helping understand the financial needs of business.

PERMANENT CURRENT ASSETS

To develop the concept of working capital, it is first necessary to understand what is meant by permanent current assets. This term ap-

---

[1] Roger K. Nordgren, "The Cornerstone of Liquidity Analysis: Working Capital," *Journal of Commercial Bank Lending*, April 1981, pp. 11-19.

pears to be self-contradicting because by definition a current asset is expected to be held for only a short time. However, some minimum amount of dollars must be invested in current assets at all times for the business to operate. There is tremendous variation from industry to industry regarding how much comprises a realistic minimum investment in current assets, but it is unlikely any business can operate with no current assets. For example, Mr. Jones (who owned the men's store discussed in Chapter 2) must have some minimum level of merchandise before opening the store. It is the dollar investment to maintain this minimum level that constitutes permanent current assets.

Frequently there will be bulges in the amount of current assets such as was the case when Mr. Smith (see Chapter 3) added Christmas merchandise to his regular inventory. These bulges should be viewed as temporary additions on top of permanent current assets. This is depicted graphically for a hypothetical firm in Figure 4-1.

Figure 4-1.   Comparison of Temporary Increases in Current Assets and Permanent Current Assets

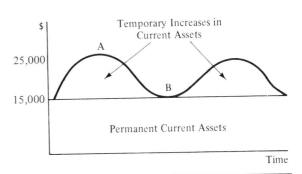

Permanent current assets refers to a minimum amount of investment in current assets necessary to conduct business rather than specific inventory items, accounts receivable or other current assets. Thus, it represents a permanent use of funds. The matching principle (see Chapter 2) states that permanent uses should be financed with permanent sources. If the firm depicted in Figure 4-1 is complying with the matching principle, then its balance sheet in abbreviated form would appear as follows at time A:

Assets			Liabilities and Owner's Equity	
Current Assets	$25,000		Current Liabilities	$10,000
Fixed Assets	75,000		Long-term Debt plus	
			Owner's Equity	90,000
Total	$100,000		Total	$100,000

Normally long-term debt and owner's equity are not combined on the balance sheet, but it serves this discussion to represent them as one amount.

At time B, the balance sheet would be as follows:

Assets			Liabilities and Owner's Equity	
Current Assets	$15,000		Long-term Debt plus	
Fixed Assets	75,000		Owner's Equity	$90,000
Total	$90,000		Total	$90,000

This company is observing the matching principle because fixed assets and permanent current assets, both representing long-term uses, are financed with long-term sources.

WORKING CAPITAL

It was pointed out earlier that working capital is measured by current assets minus current liabilities. Thus, the company being considered here has $15,000 of working capital, the amount of permanent current assets, but a meaningful definition of working capital is still lacking. However, if it is remembered that capital refers to financing *sources* while current assets represent a *use*, then a step has been taken toward developing a useful concept for working capital. It should be thought of in terms of the right side of the balance sheet, not the left side.

To be a useful concept, *working capital* should be defined as that portion of long-term sources (long-term debt and owner's equity) that finances permanent current assets. The balance sheet at point A is reconstructed to illustrate this definition.

Assets		Liabilities and Owner's Equity	
Temporary Current Assets	$ 10,000	Current Liabilities	$ 10,000
		Working Capital	15,000
Permanent Current Assets	15,000	Balance of Long-term debt plus owner's equity	
Fixed Assets	75,000		75,000
Total	$100,000	Total˙	$100,000

SIGNIFICANCE OF WORKING CAPITAL

The above balance sheet is incorrect in terms of appropriate accounting designations, but it provides a meaningful illustration of working capital as a financing concept. What is its significance to the person involved in commercial lending? The dollars representing investment in permanent current assets are otherwise unavailable, just as are the dollars invested in buildings, trucks and other fixed assets. Buildings and trucks should not be financed with short-term debt (current liabilities), nor should permanent current assets. The firm will be under constant liquidity pressures, as described in Chapter 2, if it depends on short-term sources for long-term uses. However, a great many companies place too much dependence on short-term credit; this is particularly true of growing companies.[2]

LIQUIDITY PROBLEMS OF GROWING COMPANIES

When a company grows, it not only acquires more fixed assets, but also more current assets. A larger investment is required in permanent current assets. Many growing firms recognize that they must have long-term financing for the increase in fixed assets but attempt to meet the expansion of permanent current assets by greater use of trade credit or other short-term debt. This violates the matching principle and often

---

[2] Lawrence D. Schall and Charles W. Haley, *Introduction to Financial Management* (New York, NY: McGraw-Hill, 1980), pp. 567-569.

causes a liquidity squeeze. The more rapid a firm's growth, the more the liquidity pressure it encounters. For such a firm, the best financing might be provided under revolving credit agreements.

REVOLVING CREDIT AGREEMENTS

A revolving credit agreement is an agreement in which the lender, in return for a commitment fee, agrees to have funds ready up to a pre-established amount whenever the borrower needs them. It normally extends for a period of two to three years. The agreement is legally binding on the lender, and the borrowing firm can draw and repay funds as many times as it wishes during the period of the agreement.

FEATURES OF REVOLVING CREDIT

The revolving credit agreement is formal in nature. It will specify the maximum amount that can be borrowed and the method of establishing the interest rate on amounts borrowed. The agreement also will set forth several requirements with which the borrower must comply during the term of the agreement. These requirements might include limits on how much the firm can borrow from other sources, minimum amounts of insurance to maintain and ceilings on how much owners can withdraw from the business. The lender should include every requirement in the agreement that it considers important to its own protection. Since the self-liquidating feature is lacking in loans extended under revolving credit agreements, these revolving credit agreements must be considered to be more risky as a class than the short-term loans discussed in Chapter 3. This does not mean such loans should be avoided, but that they should be designed with care and made with complete understanding as to their use.

USE OF A REVOLVING CREDIT AGREEMENT LOAN

Funds borrowed under a revolving credit agreement normally are used to finance fixed assets or permanent current assets. The borrower normally does not know exactly when funds will be needed (over the coming two- to three-year period) or how much will be needed from time to time. Most often this arrangement is made to help accommodate a firm's period of expansion.

An example of a growing firm that might make use of a revolving credit agreement would be a retail store chain that is gradually adding several new outlets. As each new outlet is completed, it is stocked with inventory, thus increasing the need for working capital. This expansion of the need for working capital is illustrated in Figure 4-2.

Figure 4-2. Expansion of Working Capital Requirement

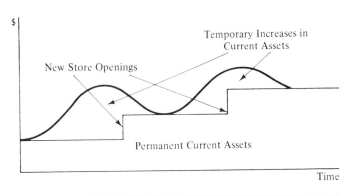

The company would continue to depend on trade credit or seasonal loans to finance temporary increases in current assets. The revolving credit would provide funds to finance the increase in permanent current assets (working capital) as well as the added amounts required to finance increases in fixed assets.

During the expansion period, the revolving credit arrangement would allow the firm to draw more funds as needed, removing the necessity of applying for a new loan each time a store was completed. And if the firm was able to pay down the balance of the loan from time to time, its interest costs would be reduced.

REPAYING THE REVOLVING LOAN

When the period of the revolving credit agreement is over, the unpaid loan balance should be replaced with permanent financing in the form of additions to owner's equity or a longer-term loan. And it is important to remember that the method of final payment should be determined at the time the revolving credit agreement is established. Too often the borrower expects (or at least hopes) loan repayment will be made from increased profits during the expansion period. However, few companies can increase profits rapidly enough to meet liquidity needs and provide the permanent financing to carry fixed assets and the permanent increase in current assets during a period of growth. Therefore, it is frequently a provision of a revolving credit agreement that any unpaid balance at the agreement's expiration will automatically be replaced by a term loan.

TERM LOANS

Term loans finance long-term uses, including permanent current assets, and usually mature in no more than seven years. They often stem from revolving credit agreements. When the revolving credit agreement expires, the firm should know its longer-term credit needs. The term loan, with its specified repayment schedule, is then more appropriate.

Term loans are important as sources of capital to companies that are too small to sell bonds in the capital markets. Large firms also use term loans when the amount needed is too small to justify a bond issue or if the period for which funds are needed is shorter than that for which bonds normally are issued.[3]

Term lending is much more complex than short-term lending. The term loan requires extensive credit analysis, projection of future years' results, management assessment, documentation and other considerations that may enter into short-term lending to only a limited degree.

PROVISIONS OF TERM LOANS

Frequently, collateral is more common for term loans than short-term loans. Term loans do not enjoy the self-liquidating feature, and there is more uncertainty associated with longer periods of time. Repayment normally is in installments. Payments may be set quarterly or even annually to match the cash flow pattern of a business. This is often the arrangement with agricultural term lending, with payments set to coincide with income from crops.

The balloon payment is a common feature of term loans. A large part, perhaps 40 to 50 percent, of the loan comprises the balloon and is scheduled as the final payment. If the borrower has met all earlier payments as scheduled and has good prospects, the balloon probably will be rolled into a new term loan if the borrower so wishes. The balloon payment at the end serves to keep payments low in the early years of a term loan, giving the borrower more flexibility.

---

[3] Edward W. Reed et al, *Commercial Banking*, 2nd edition (Englewood Cliffs, NJ: Prentice Hall, 1980), pp. 282-284.

Term loans should be distinguished from mortgage loans on business buildings and installment loans on equipment. All three are for longer-term uses and all three are retired with installment payments. Mortgages are normally longer term, however, and both mortgages and installment loans usually attach only to specific assets which in turn serve as collateral for the loans.

A single term loan may provide the financing for more than one purpose, including an increase in permanent current assets. Other assets besides those financed may be required as collateral. Also, the term loan agreement usually is much more restrictive than a mortgage or installment loan contract.

TERM LOAN AGREEMENTS

The *term loan agreement* sets forth the purpose of the loan, repayment provisions, method of interest rate determination, various pieces of information about the borrower and the collateral, if any, that secures the loan. It also contains various "affirmative" covenants. These are requirements to be met by the borrower, such as providing annual and quarterly financial statements, maintaining a certain level of working capital, carrying adequate insurance, keeping fixed assets in good repair and paying all taxes.

Another section of the term loan agreement consists of "negative" covenants, that is, certain things which the borrower will not do. For example, a negative covenant could state that dividends will not be increased during the period of the term loan, or that other indebtedness cannot be incurred without the concurrence of the term lender. A negative covenant may limit the investments the firm can make or restrict prepayment of other debts. Sales of assets also may be restricted, and restrictions may be placed on entering into leases.

The term loan agreement will also define those events that would constitute default, making the entire loan immediately due and payable. The most obvious of these would be failure to make interest and principal payments when due, but failure to meet any of the affirmative or negative covenants may also constitute default. Voluntary or involuntary bankruptcy also will constitute default. And if any of the representations and warranties made by the borrower in the term loan agreement are false, the loan may be declared in default. Examples of representations and warranties would be that the borrower has no pending lawsuits, that financial statements are correct and that all taxes are current.

The term loan agreement is in many cases a complex document, prepared by the lender's attorneys, and intended to provide protection to the lender. Previous discussions in this book have brought out the point that a firm's liquidity can be exhausted very rapidly, a risk which falls heavily on the term lender. It may appear to be an onerous document which is very restrictive for the borrower. It should be no more restrictive than necessary to serve its purpose. That purpose is to ensure continued liquidity in the borrower's balance sheet so that payments of principal and interest can be made as scheduled.

SMALL BUSINESS ADMINISTRATION GUARANTEED LOANS

The Small Business Administration (SBA) is an agency of the federal government responsible for improving opportunities for small businesses through various programs. One of these programs includes guarantee of loans made to a small business if the business meets the Small Business Administration requirements. One of these requirements is that the firm must show that it could not acquire the loan under reasonable terms without the Small Business Administration guarantee.

Prior to making application for a Small Business Administration guaranteed loan, the potential borrower first must attempt to obtain a loan through normal procedures from a financial institution. If the borrower is refused credit, or if the interest rate that would apply is excessive, then, usually after three such turn downs, application may be made for a Small Business Administration guaranteed loan.

The loan application is made to a financial intermediary using forms supplied by the Small Business Administration. The financial intermediary sends the application to the Small Business Administration and, on approval, makes the loan.

Interest rate limits are set by the Small Business Administration, but these are quite lenient. Floating rates are allowed. A lender can charge a rate related to the prime rate and based on the loan term. For example, a loan with a term of more than seven years may carry a rate up to 2-3/4 percent over the prime; for a loan with a term less than seven years, the rate may be 2-1/4 percent over the prime.

The Small Business Administration guarantees the lender that it will repay 90 percent of the loan up to $500,000 in the event of default. This minimizes the risk to the lender while enabling it to supply capital to businesses. The guarantee also injects liquidity into the loan. Many lenders sell the 90 percent guaranteed portion of loans to long-term investors, such as pension funds. The guaranteed portion is a very high quality investment since it is guaranteed by the federal government. The lender retains the other 10 percent of the loan, but continues to collect payment for the entire loan. The lender receives a service fee for the portion of the payment collected and remitted to the long-term investor.

The Farmer's Home Administration has a similar guarantee program for business loans made in rural communities. Many small financial intermediaries prefer Small Business Administration and Farmer's Home Administration lending because it removes most of the credit risk from intermediate-term business loans. The liquidity provided by the secondary market for the guaranteed portions of Small Business Administration loans is also very important, and many lenders make Small Business Administration loans with the intent of selling the guaranteed 90 percent. This prevents "locking up" large amounts of the financial intermediary's funds in longer-term loans while allowing it to build good deposit and other relationships with the business borrowers. It is a reasonable expectation that the borrower will maintain deposits with the lender.

INTERMEDIATE-TERM FARM LOANS

Successful lending to any form of business requires an understanding of the nature of the business, and this is particularly true for farming. To add to the complexities created by weather conditions and sharp price changes, farming is often the victim of political decision making. The Russian wheat boycott of the late 1970s is an example.

When one farmer is in difficulty, many may be. Thus, the value of used equipment (which may have been new when the lender advanced funds to buy it) may plummet. If beef prices drop, the perfectly healthy livestock which the financial intermediary financed may suddenly be worth less than the balance that they secure.

Farming is a capital-intensive business. In order to raise capital, many farmers borrow against their farm real estate. Other forms of collateral for intermediate-term loans include equipment and livestock (other than feeder livestock). Such loans may or may not take the form of term loans.

LEASING

Many business firms meet part or all of their intermediate-term credit needs by leasing fixed assets. Essentially they borrow the assets rather than borrow the money to buy the assets. While there are some legal and tax differences which may make leasing more appealing than a mortgage or an equipment installment loan, the purpose, having the asset to use in the business, is the same. Leased business assets range from office equipment and small machinery to major items such as large computers and airplanes.

FORMS OF LEASES

A lease is a contract wherein the owner of an asset, the lessor, authorizes use of the asset by another, the lessee. The lease sets the period of use, amount and timing of payments, maintenance responsibility, insurance and other requirements. For an operating lease, the lessor usually provides maintenance, insurance and pays the property tax, if any. Operating leases normally are for short periods, seldom exceeding three years, and are cancellable.

Financial intermediaries normally do not enter into operating leases. They usually limit leasing activity to "financial leases." A financial lease normally covers several years and cannot be cancelled. Also, full payout of the asset usually takes place during the life of a financial lease. Full payout means the payments over the life of the lease return the full cost of the asset to the lessor plus a rate of return on the funds invested in the asset.

A leveraged lease is a form of financial lease which brings in another party–a long-term lender–who provides part of the financing in addition to the portion provided by the lessor. The long-term funds are borrowed by the lessor on a nonrecourse basis with the leased assets providing security for the loan. This arrangement allows lessors to engage in a greater volume of leasing activity with a given amount of capital. The lessor normally earns a fee as well for originating the lease.

REASONS FOR LEASING

Leasing is a very complex activity and should be entered into by any financial intermediary only after development of a sufficient level of expertise. The benefits of leasing to the intermediary can include:

- Better rates of return by leasing assets rather than by lending to buy the same assets.
- Diversification, both in terms of services offered and in terms of adding fixed assets to its balance sheet.
- A competitive tool to help expand overall business.

Businesses which lease cite several advantages, not all of which are applicable in each situation. Leasing

- conserves cash because no down payment is required under a lease;

- allows indirect benefit of the investment tax credit (through lower lease payments) for firms that are not sufficiently profitable to enjoy direct benefit;
- avoids many of the limitations of loan agreements;
- conserves borrowing capacity for other uses;
- provides a tax advantage due to full deductibility of lease payments.

The Economic Recovery Tax Act of 1981 made the rules governing leasing much simpler. Comparing these with prior rules is beyond the scope of this text, but it should be mentioned that prior to the Act a lease could be interpreted by the Internal Revenue Service as an installment contract if it did not meet a number of specific provisions. As an installment contract any tax benefits were lost.

The Act defined a so-called "safe harbor" lease as one in which:

- Both lessor and lessee agree the arrangement is a lease.
- The lessor must be a corporation.
- The lessor must have a ten percent investment in the asset throughout the life of the asset.
- The term of the lease must meet a test based on the life of the asset.

LIQUIDITY VERSUS CASH FLOW AND PROFITABILITY

Liquidity and cash flow were defined in Chapter 2. In Chapter 3, it was pointed out that the lender looked to the self-liquidating feature of the loan for repayment much more so than to the profits a business might earn from selling its merchandise. This is another way of saying that liquidity (both that of the asset financed and in the balance sheet—see Chapter 2) is of primary concern in short-term lending. However, profitability and cash flow are more important in intermediate-term lending.

Cash flow was defined in Chapter 2 as net income plus noncash expenses for a given period. For a company, cash flow for a period is the amount of cash the firm can generate without reducing assets (except by depreciation charges or other noncash expenses) or increasing liabilities or owner's equity. Therefore, since intermediate-term loans (for fixed assets or permanent investment in current assets) are not self-liquidating, the lender must look to cash flow of the firm over the years of the loan as the ultimate source of repayment. However, a total reliance on cash flow, with no separate regard for the net income portion of cash flow, can be dangerous. For example, the equipment a firm might use to conduct its activities must be replaced from time to time. If cash flow consists entirely of depreciation write-offs, then it must be presumed that new loans are required each time a machine is replaced. The firm makes no headway, and, in fact, falls behind in inflationary periods because each loan will be larger than the previous one. Moreover, throughout the entire process there is nothing provided to the owners as return on their investment because there have been no profits. Sooner or later illiquidity is bound to reach problem proportions and loan repayment may lag. Thus, in looking to cash flow for repayment, the need for a reasonable profit must be included.

The lender should view making a term loan as almost equivalent to entering into partnership with the borrower. The lender should not make the loan unless there is confidence it will help the borrower's profit performance, just as no business partnership will be formed unless there are good expectations for success.

NEED FOR INTERMEDIATE-TERM LOANS

The U.S. economy has experienced unusually high rates of inflation since the 1960s. This means that inventory items and fixed assets purchased by companies continue to increase in price. Many firms cannot generate profits at a sufficient rate to provide the long-term capital needed for investment in fixed assets and permanent current assets. Thus, a need for added amounts of intermediate-term (and/or long-term) credit is generated as a result of inflation. If a firm is experiencing rapid growth in sales volume, this need is even more acute.

SUMMARY

Intermediate-term loans have stated repayment periods spanning more than one year and are made to finance long-term uses. Besides fixed assets, long-term uses also include permanent current assets. Permanent current assets is the term used to describe the investment in current assets necessary for basic operation of a firm.

Permanent current assets represent a long-term use of financing and, therefore, should be financed by a long-term source. That portion of long-term capital that provides the financing of permanent current assets is working capital. It is computed by subtracting current liabilities from current assets.

If permanent current assets are not financed with long-term sources, the firm is subject to liquidity shortages. This problem is particularly difficult for growing firms to avoid because they cannot add to owner's equity through profits as rapidly as they acquire new fixed assets and add to the level of permanent current assets.

The revolving credit agreement normally covers two to three years. It allows the borrowing firm to draw funds up to a specified amount and make partial repayment as it wishes during the life of the agreement. A commitment fee of 1/4 to 1/2 percent of the maximum amount is normal. Revolving credit agreements often fund into term loans.

Term loans are made to finance long-term assets and permanent current assets. Repayment is on an installment basis, often including a balloon at the end. The complexity and potential risk in term lending may require an extensive term loan agreement to protect the lender.

The Small Business Administration guarantees up to 90 percent of the principal of qualifying loans made by financial institutions to small firms. The guaranteed portion may be sold to long-term investors at the discretion of the lender.

Farming requires extensive amounts of capital for equipment, livestock and other purposes. Lending to farmers requires an extensive understanding of farm operations.

Leasing is a form of intermediate-term credit. With leasing, assets are borrowed rather than money which in turn is used to buy the assets. Numerous advantages, many of them tax related, are cited for leasing rather than borrowing to purchase.

While the borrower's liquidity is of greatest importance to a lender when short-term credit is extended, cash flow is most important in intermediate-term lending. However, the lender should not place excessive emphasis on the depreciation portion of cash flow. Profitability is essential and helping increase profitability should be the basic justification for extending intermediate-term credit.

CHAPTER QUESTIONS

1. Although the term "permanent current assets" sounds self-contradicting, it has a specific meaning. What is it?
2. Define working capital in terms of the right side of the balance sheet.

3. Why do many profitable, rapidly growing companies have liquidity problems?

4. What is a revolving credit agreement and how might it be used by a business firm?

5. What are some of the purposes for which a term loan might be granted?

6. What are four covenants which might appear in a term loan agreement?

7. Why is leasing considered a form of intermediate-term financing?

8. What is "cash flow" and why is it considered the source of repayment of intermediate-term loans?

5

Financial
Statement Analysis

OBJECTIVES

After reading Chapter 5, you should be able to:

- State the purpose of financial statement analysis;
- Describe ratio analysis;
- Name four categories of ratios and at least one ratio in each category;
- Explain the process of interpreting ratios;
- Describe breakeven analysis and explain its purpose;
- Discuss the process of spreading financial statements;
- Give examples of methods of financial projection.

The basic business financial statements were described in Chapter 2. Chapters 3 and 4 discussed various types of short- and intermediate-term credit used by business firms. With the background provided by those chapters, attention can now be given to the process of analyzing the financial statements of business firms.

The purpose of financial statement analysis is to learn as much as possible from the statements about the financial strengths and weaknesses of a company. This knowledge is important in the process that leads to the decision to grant or not to grant credit to a firm. It is also valuable in helping the company determine what kind of loan is most appropriate and how much it can justifiably borrow. In addition, financial statement analysis is important in keeping abreast of developing conditions within a company after a loan is made.

The focus of this chapter is on the fundamentals of statement analysis. Other considerations in the credit granting process, including those that may be unique to a particular company or industry, are discussed in Chapter 8.

APPROACH TO STATEMENT ANALYSIS

Before undertaking the analysis of a set of financial statements, it is important to decide what specific questions the analyst wants to answer. Since there are many approaches and techniques that may be applied to analyzing statements, there is a danger of producing numbers and comparisons that are more confusing than enlightening. If the analyst has a clear concept of what he or she is looking for in the statements, the choice of analytical methods is simplified.[1]

Second, the analyst must recognize that the statements are historical in nature. The information the statements provide may not be applicable to future periods if significant changes have recently occurred in the company or the economy. The analysis may only help in the formation of other questions that should be answered through personal interviews with the customer or visits to the customer's place of business.

A third consideration is to recognize the tremendous variation that exists from one company's statements to another's. This may be due to industry differences, size of company, type of business formation

---

[1] Erich A. Helfert, *Techniques of Financial Analysis*, 4th edition (Homewood, IL: Richard D. Irwin, Inc., 1977), Chapter 2.

or other reasons, all of which the analyst must consider. Also, there is a great deal of latitude that may be applied in the preparation of statements. This latitude was first mentioned in Chapter 2 when the importance of footnotes and the auditor's report were mentioned. A careful review of all footnotes is essential to a thorough understanding of the statements.

RATIO ANALYSIS

Ratio analysis is a basic form of financial analysis. If a company's financial statements are comprehensive, professionally prepared and current, a significant understanding of the company can be developed with ratio analysis. It must be recognized, however, that ratio analysis seldom provides final answers. Instead, it is a rapid and inexpensive method of narrowing the focus of a credit analysis to a few pertinent questions.

Some ratios can be calculated from any set of comprehensive statements. The analyst must learn to select those which are most meaningful in a given situation. The ratios calculated below are generally considered important. They fall into four categories: liquidity, asset management, financial leverage and profitability. The balance sheet and income statement (see Figure 5-1) of the hypothetical Brown Corporation will be used to illustrate computation of the ratios.

Figure 5-1. Balance Sheet and Income Statement for the Brown Corporation— December 31, 198A

The Brown Coporation
Balance Sheet - December 31, 198A

Assets		Liabilities and Owner's Equity	
Current Assets			
Cash	$10,000	Accounts Payable	$25,000
Marketable		Accrued Expenses	15,000
Securities	20,000		
		Mortgage Loan	20,000
Accounts			
Receivable	20,000	Term Loan	15,000
Inventories	30,000	Paid In Capital	25,000

Fixed Assets		Retained Earnings	50,000
Plant and Equipment	100,000	Total	$150,000
Less Accumu-lated Depre-ciation	(30,000)		
Total	$150,000		

The Brown Corporation
Income Statement - Year Ended December 31, 198A

Sales		$450,000
Cost of goods sold		300,000
Gross margin on sales		$150,000
Operating Expenses		
Selling expenses	$ 25,000	
General and administrative	96,000	
Total operating expenses		$121,000
Income from operations		$ 29,000
Other income (interest on loans)		3,000
Total income		$ 32,000
Less other expenses (interest on loans)		4,000
Income before taxes		$ 28,000
Income taxes (50%)		14,000
Net income		$ 14,000
Dividends paid		7,000
Increase in retained earnings		$ 7,000

LIQUIDITY RATIOS

The concept of liquidity was defined in Chapter 2 in terms of a single asset and a company's balance sheet. In Chapter 3 it was pointed out that liquidity, as it related to assets turning into cash through the cash cycle, was more important in making short-term loans than whether or not the firm made a profit on the specific items financed. Therefore, it stands to reason that liquidity ratios would be most important in the short-term lending process. Two liquidity ratios are commonly calculated: current ratio and acidtest ratio.

Current Ratio

The most common indicator of a company's ability to meet short-term obligations is the *current ratio*. It is computed by dividing current assets by current liabilities. In the case of the Brown Corporation, the computation would be:

$$\text{Current Ratio} = \frac{\text{Current Assets}}{\text{Current Liabilities}} = \frac{\$80,000}{\$40,000} = 2$$

The current ratio of 2 means that $2 worth of current assets (in the form of cash and liquid assets which can be converted to cash in a short period of time) are available to cover each $1 of short-term obligations in the form of current liabilities. Or, looking at this ratio from a different perspective, current assets could experience "shrinkage" of 50 percent before they were inadequate to cover current liabilities. Of course, an operating business never liquidates all of its current assets at one time and pays off all of its current liabilities, but if the ratio is too low, a given company may be under constant pressure to meet its payments.

For example, the commercial lender contemplating making a seasonal inventory loan should be very concerned if the firm's current ratio is low. If it is low and the loan is made, the borrower may use cash received from selling the inventory to pay other short-term debts rather than repay the seasonal loan; even though this was not necessarily the intent of the borrower at the time the loan was made. It might have been the borrower's belief that all short-term obligations could be met, including repayment of the seasonal loan. However, if business was not as good as hoped, and other creditors were placing pressure on the borrower, then funds might have gone to pay debts other than the seasonal loan.

Diversion of the proceeds from sale of the inventory to pay other debts could place the commercial lender in an undesirable position. The borrower is unable to repay the seasonal loan when due and the inventory has been sold. The lender may be faced with taking a longer-term note in place of the short-term obligation thus obtaining whatever collateral, if any, may be left unpledged.

Acid Test Ratio

The current ratio does not take into account the lack of liquidity of many types of inventory. Some inventory items may be old and outdated. Their sale might be possible only at prices far below their book value on the balance sheet. In the case of a manufacturing firm, much of the inventory may be work in process, so instant marketability would be severely limited.

Financial analysts use the *acid test ratio* (sometimes called the quick ratio) as a more stringent indicator of the ability to meet near-term obligations. It excludes inventory from the computation. For the Brown Corporation the acid test ratio is:

$$\text{Acid Test Ratio} = \frac{\text{Current Assets} - \text{Inventory}}{\text{Current Liabilities}} = \frac{\$50,000}{\$40,000} = 1.25$$

As is true of all ratios, whether the acid test ratio is too low or not depends on a number of considerations including what is considered standard for the industry. Industry averages are discussed later in the chapter.

ASSET MANAGEMENT RATIOS

Management effectiveness in several areas can be indicated by asset management ratios, sometimes called activity ratios. Three will be defined below: inventory turnover, average collection period and asset turnover.

Inventory Turnover

The inventory turnover ratio is computed by dividing cost of goods sold for the year by the average inventory during the year. It is important to use average rather than year-end inventory because at year-end the inventory may be at a seasonal high or low. The average inventory can be calculated from interim statements or monthly inventory records if these are available. Here it will be assumed the Brown Corporation year-end inventory is the same as its average inventory for the year. Thus, the inventory turnover is:

$$\text{Inventory Turnover} = \frac{\text{Cost of Goods Sold}}{\text{Average Inventory}} = \frac{\$300,000}{\$30,000} = 10x$$

The larger the ratio the "faster" inventory moved through the firm and the shorter the time dollars were tied up in specific items of inventory. The larger the ratio the better up to a point. If it is much too high then the firm probably is working with an insufficient level of inventory. It could improve sales with more inventory. If the ratio is too low, then too much money is tied up in slow-moving inventory. The lender should refer to industry averages as an aid in determining whether or not one company's ratio is "too high" or "too low."

Average Collection Period

If a company extends credit to its customers and if many of the customers are very slow to make payment, a large amount of money can be tied up in slow paying receivables. To calculate the average collection period it is necessary to know the average credit sales per day. This figure can be computed if the credit sales for the year are known. It is assumed all of the Brown Corporation sales are credit sales, so:

$$\text{Average credit sales per day} = \frac{\text{Annual Credit Sales}}{365}$$

$$= \frac{\$450,000}{365} = \$1,233$$

then,

$$\text{Average collection period} = \frac{\text{Accounts Receivable}}{\text{Credit Sales Per Day}}$$

$$= \frac{\$20,000}{\$1,233} = 16.2 \text{ days}$$

This example also assumes that year-end accounts receivable are the same as average accounts receivable during the year.

If the average collection period is too long, the firm may be selling to financially weak customers in order to bolster sales. The benefit of increased sales volume may be more than offset by losses due to uncollected receivables and the lost earning power of large amounts of money tied up in slow paying receivables.

Asset Turnover

This ratio indicates how well the total investment in assets is being utilized to generate sales. If the company has a large investment in low productivity assets, the ratio will be low. The ratio for the Brown Corporation is:

$$\text{Asset Turnover} = \frac{\text{Sales}}{\text{Total Assets}} = \frac{\$450,000}{\$150,000} = 3X$$

FINANCIAL LEVERAGE RATIOS

Financial leverage was defined in Chapter 2 as the effect on earnings brought about by the use of debt. Companies borrow to try to improve the rate of return on owner's equity. Use of leverage imposes financial risk, so the analyst should try to assess that risk. Three ratios that are useful in that effort are: total debt to total assets, funded debt to owner's equity and times interest earned.

Total Debt to Total Assets

This ratio is referred to frequently as the *debt ratio*. As long as a company has owner's equity on the balance sheet and some debt, the number will be between 0 and 1. The higher the ratio the greater the company's overall dependence on debt and the greater the risk that at some future time the company will not be able to meet scheduled debt payments. The ratio for the Brown Corporation is calculated as follows:

$$\text{Total debt to total assets} = \frac{\text{Total Debt}}{\text{Total Assets}} = \frac{\$75,000}{\$150,000} = .5$$

Funded Debt to Owner's Equity

Funded debt includes intermediate- and long-term debt, that is, all debt other than current liabilities. Funded debt plus owner's equity comprise the *capital structure* of the firm, that is, the long-term commitment to the business. If only a small proportion of that commitment is provided by owners, then their willingness to stay with the company through difficult times may be limited. This ratio for the Brown Corporation is computed as follows:

$$\text{Funded Debt to Owner's Equity} = \frac{\text{Funded Debt}}{\text{Owner's Equity}}$$

$$= \frac{\$35,000}{\$75,000} = .47$$

Times Interest Earned

An important question to the analyst is how much earnings can decline before the company can no longer meet fixed interest payments. This ratio for the Brown Corporation is:

$$\text{Times Interest Earned} = \frac{\text{Total Income}}{\text{Interest Expense}} = \frac{\$32,000}{\$4,000} = 8x$$

Total income is income before interest and taxes. This amount comprises the income available to pay interest because interest is a tax deductible expense. In other words, if total income had been only $4,000 instead of $32,000, the entire amount would have been used to pay interest expense. Net income and taxes would have been zero.

This ratio includes only fixed interest expense. In many cases the analyst will want to compute the more comprehensive version of the ratio which includes principal payments on debt plus other fixed charges such as lease payments. This comprehensive version is called the *fixed-charges coverage ratio*.

PROFITABILITY RATIOS

The commercial loan officer contemplating extending longer-term credit to a company must be particularly concerned with profitability. The first profitability ratio given below is in terms of sales. How effective is the company in retaining a portion of each sales dollar for the owners? It is the firm's net margin.

Two additional ratios also are introduced: return on assets and return on owner's equity. The first defines profitability in terms of the total assets of the firm and the second in terms of the investment by the owners.

Net Margin

The net margin ratio might be termed return on sales. It is computed for the Brown Corporation as follows:

$$\text{Net Margin} = \frac{\text{Net Income}}{\text{Sales}} = \frac{\$14,000}{\$450,000} = 3.1\%$$

This ratio shows that of every $1 of sales, the owners were able to keep just over 3 cents. In the case of the Brown Corporation, owners received half of that 3.1 percent in the form of dividends while the other half was reinvested in the business.

Whether or not a net margin of 3.1 percent is good or bad depends on the characteristics of the industry in which the Brown Corporation operates. Some industries characteristically have low margins and others high margins.

Return on Assets

The *return on assets ratio* indicates how well the total investment in assets is being utilized on behalf of the owners. Not only should this ratio be compared to industry averages, but also with rates of return from other possible alternative assets. The Brown Corporation's return on assets is:

$$\text{Return on Assets} = \frac{\text{Net Income}}{\text{Assets}} = \frac{\$14,000}{\$150,000} = 9.3\%$$

This does not mean the owners earned 9.3 percent on their investments. This would have been the case only if the company were completely financed by equity capital, that is, it made no use of debt. How effectively debt was used to increase the return to the owners on their investment above 9.3 percent is shown by the return on equity ratio.

Return on Equity

The owners of a company want to earn a good rate of return on the funds they have invested in the company. The *return on equity ratio* is the measure of the success of the effort to earn a profit and is thus the most important ratio computed. The return can be compared with the return from any alternative use which the owners might have made of their funds. For example, if the rate is consistently lower than the return which the owners could have experienced by owning Treasury bills, then it might be concluded that the investment in the company has not been very beneficial. Of course, it is not the intent of the owners to continuously earn less than they could from Treasury bills or other high quality, liquid assets. If the ratio is low, the analyst should investigate further to try to determine the potential for improvement. Return on equity for the Brown Corporation is:

$$\text{Return on Equity} = \frac{\text{Net Income}}{\text{Owner's Equity}} = \frac{\$14,000}{\$75,000} = 18.7\%$$

This ratio can be compared with results that might be achieved with alternative investment opportunities.

INTERPRETING RATIOS

A ratio conveys little information unless it can be compared to some standard or average. After he or she gains experience in commercial lending and ratio analysis, the commercial lending officer will have opinions as to how high or low ratios should be to be considered acceptable. If a ratio is too high or low, further evaluation should be conducted before conclusions are drawn.

Besides relying on his or her experience to judge ratios, the analyst should employ other forms of comparison. The most common method is to compare ratios with industry averages. This does not mean that conformance with the industry average is a requirement, but any major departure from the industry average does suggest the need for additional investigation.

RATIO PROFILE

All of the previous ratios calculated for the Brown Corporation may be considered to form a ratio profile for the company at a given point in time. Figure 5-2 lists those ratios and the average ratios for other companies in the same industry.

Figure 5-2. Comparison of Brown Corporation Ratios with Industry Averages as of December 31, 198A

Ratio	Brown Corp.	Industry Av.
Current Ratio	2	3
Acid Test Ratio	1.25	1.0
Inventory Turnover	10x	6x
Average Collection Period	16.2 days	20.2 days
Asset Turnover	3x	2.5x
Total Debt to Total Assets	.5	.6
Funded Debt to Owner's Equity	.47	.55
Times Interest Earned	8x	6x
Net Margin	3.1%	2.8%
Return on Assets	9.3%	8.6%
Return on Equity	18.7%	19.2%

The comparison with industry average ratios suggests that the Brown Corporation is not distinctly different from the typical company in the industry. However, some of the individual comparisons are noteworthy. First, Brown's current ratio is below average but its acid test ratio is above average. That suggests working capital is low, that is, there is fairly heavy reliance on current liabilities to finance current assets. A portion of permanent current assets probably is financed with current liabilities (see the discussion of working capital in Chapter 4).

Next, it should be noted that Brown's inventory turnover is faster than average. Perhaps Brown is unusually efficient in its inventory management, but perhaps inventory levels are so low that some sales opportunities are missed. Raising that question could lead to the question of the purpose of the $20,000 of marketable securities held by Brown.   The analyst may suggest that these funds could be more profitably employed if invested in additional inventory.

The financial leverage ratios indicate Brown has less debt burden than the average company in the industry. Comparison of Brown's return on assets with its return on equity suggests that some increase in return on equity could be gained with a moderate increase in intermediate- or long-term debt without overloading the company with financial risk.

If the analysis of the Brown Corporation was undertaken due to an application by the company for an intermediate-term, working capital loan to be used to expand inventory, then the ratios would tend to support the application. The loan would improve the current ratio (increase working capital) and presumably improve sales opportunities. A moderate debt addition should not be difficult for the firm to carry.

If, however, the Brown Corporation is applying for short-term credit, the ratios do not suggest support for the application. If investigation beyond the ratios did not provide a different view, then it might be recommended to the company that it consider another term loan.

INDUSTRY RATIOS

Each industry has unique characteristics which influence the balance sheet and income statement values of firms in the industry. These in turn result in average industry ratios that may be significantly different from average ratios in other industries. Retail food stores, for example, usually have a large amount of their assets represented by inventory, but have few if any receivables. The acid-test ratio for a grocery store could reasonably be expected to be much lower than that for an equipment wholesaler that makes a large proportion of its sales on credit.

It is very helpful for the analyst to compare the ratios he or she has calculated with industry averages. If the company's ratios are distinctly different from industry averages, the next step is to determine the reason.

There are several sources of average ratios, and one or more of these should be acquired by the analyst. The one most used by commercial lenders is the *Annual Statement Studies* published by Robert Morris Associates.[2] The 1981 edition included ratios for 321 industries. Sixteen ratios were calculated for each industry with industries subdivided into size categories. In addition, each ratio is presented at three levels: for the median firm, the upper quartile (top fourth) and lower quartile (bottom fourth) within each industry subgroup.

Another source of ratios is the *Almanac of Business and Industrial Financial Ratios* which is published annually by Prentice-Hall, Inc. *The Quarterly Financial Report for U.S. Manufacturing Corporations* is another source. It is published jointly by the Federal Trade Commission and the Securities and Exchange Commission. Other government agencies such as the Small Business Administration and the Commerce Department are sources of information which include ratios and some trade associations provide ratios for members of their respective industries.

---

[2] Robert Morris Associates, Philadelphia, PA, is an association of commercial bank commercial loan officers.

COMBINING RATIOS

Each separate ratio might be regarded as a piece of a puzzle. It has some meaning by itself, but this meaning is expanded when it is combined with other ratios.

Trend Analysis

A ratio for the most recent period can be combined with the same ratio for previous periods to see if there is some suggestion of developing problems. If a ratio has increased (or decreased) steadily for several periods, a trend may have developed that should be reversed. For example, if the average collection period has increased as follows, the company may be granting increasing volumes of credit to customers who may be financially weak in order to maintain or increase sales.

	1979	1980	1981	1982
XYZ Company	13 days	15 days	21 days	29 days
Industry Average	16 days	15 days	16 days	17 days

If so, sooner or later some large losses may result and write-offs of receivables will be taken. The company's liquidity may be less than its current balance sheet suggests and its net worth essentially is overstated.

Margin, Turnover and Return on Assets

The relationship between net margin and asset turnover is very important and should be understood by anyone making business loans. Earlier in this chapter net margin was defined as net income divided by sales, and asset turnover was defined as sales divided by total assets. A third ratio, return on assets, was defined as net income divided by total assets. The relationship among these three ratios can be expressed as follows:

$$\frac{\text{Net Income}}{\text{Sales}} \times \frac{\text{Sales}}{\text{Total Assets}} = \frac{\text{Net Income}}{\text{Total Assets}}$$

And for the Brown Corporation:

$$\frac{\$14,000}{\$450,000} \times \frac{\$450,000}{\$150,000} = \frac{\$14,000}{\$150,000} = 9.3\%$$

Stated another way:

Net Margin x Asset Turnover = Return on Assets

And for the Brown Corporation:

$$3.1\% \times 3 = 9.3\%$$

This very important relationship helps provide an understanding of business profitability. *Profitability* (return on assets) is a result of the firm's ability to retain a portion of each sales dollar (net margin) multiplied by the firm's effectiveness in using its assets to generate sales (asset turnover). For example, how much would return on assets be increased if Brown's assets turnover were raised from 3x to 4x? Or if net margin were improved from 3.1 percent to 4.1 percent?

It is characteristic in some industries that companies will tend to have low net margins and high asset turnover ratios. In other industries the reverse is true. An example of the first would be the retail grocery industry. Margins frequently fall below one percent but asset turnover is very high because of the large volume of inventory moving through most grocery stores.

Jewelry stores, on the other hand, would be more likely to have higher net margins, perhaps 4 or 5 percent, but asset turnover is much lower. As a general rule, if a large investment in assets (fixed and/or current) is required relative to sales volume, asset turnover will tend to be low and net margins will tend to be high. The reverse usually holds true where lower asset investment is required.

LOOKING BEHIND THE RATIOS

Ratios can be helpful tools, partly because their computation is so convenient. Seldom, however, should ratios provide the sole basis for a yes or no decision regarding a loan application. Ratios should be used in combination with all of the other information about the firm and its management before a conclusion is reached. In addition, the ratios themselves may suggest points of further investigation.

For example, if a company had a return on assets ratio in line with the industry average, it might be concluded that the company was operating with no serious problems. If, however, the asset turnover ratio was significantly higher than average and the net margin was much lower than average (even though the product of the two was an average return on assets), some questions should be considered. Some possible questions are: Why is the company relatively ineffective in retaining a portion of each sales dollar? Why does it appear to be relatively effective in using its assets to generate sales?

Further investigation might reveal that the company does not compete well in its industry due to problems with its products. Thus, the low net margin results. Also, it might be found that the high asset turnover ratio results because the book value of fixed assets (plant and equipment) is unusually low. It is low because assets are old and have been written down (depreciated) to very low book values. The old, partially obsolete plant may be the reason for the company's inferior product. The company may soon require some long-term capital in order to remain competitive, if, in fact, it is not too late. The "red flag" raised by a low margin and high turnover ratio may help the analyst direct his or her investigation of an important problem area.

BREAKEVEN ANALYSIS

Some industries are more vulnerable to an economic recession than are others, and within a given industry some firms suffer more than others when a recession results in reduced sales levels. In many cases the analyst needs to know how vulnerable a company is to economic reverses or any other cause of a decline in sales in order to judge the risk involved in making a loan. Breakeven analysis indicates the degree to which profits can decline with a given decline in sales.

OPERATING LEVERAGE

Financial leverage was defined in Chapter 2 as the result attained by using borrowed funds. Borrowed funds inject a cost, interest, which must be paid before any earnings are available to owners. Operating leverage is the result of fixed costs which must be paid by the firm no matter what its production or sales level.

Fixed Costs
Examples of fixed costs are rent, depreciation, officers' salaries, insurance, interest and property taxes. These are not irrevocably fixed, of course. Rents may increase, officers can be fired and debt paid off. However, for a given period, say the next year, if the analyst is trying to estimate the level of sales required to break even, then it is appropriate to assume these costs will be paid regardless of the sales volume.

Variable Costs
Some expenses go up or down automatically with production; for example, raw materials used, electricity used by equipment, labor used in production and transportation expense. These costs can be measured as so many dollars or cents per unit of output. And, just as few costs are absolutely fixed, few costs vary perfectly with output. Some electricity will be used, no doubt, even if the plant is idle. However, the tendency

for some costs to vary and some to be fixed makes breakeven analysis an important analytical tool.

Breakeven Point

Two companies will be used to illustrate breakeven analysis and operating leverage. Company A makes a product which it sells for $1 each. Its fixed costs total $100,000 and its variable costs are 60 cents per unit. Company B also sells its product for $1 but it has fixed costs of $300,000 and variable costs are 30 cents per unit. The first step in breakeven analysis is to compute before-tax profit at several possible levels of sales. This is done in Figure 5-3.

Figure 5-3. Cost and Profit Schedules

Company A

Sales Dollars and Units	Fixed Cost	Variable Cost	Total Cost	Pretax Profit or Loss
100,000	$100,000	60,000	160,000	(60,000)
150,000	100,000	90,000	190,000	(40,000)
200,000	100,000	120,000	220,000	(20,000)
250,000	100,000	150,000	250,000	-0-
300,000	100,000	180,000	280,000	20,000
350,000	100,000	210,000	310,000	40,000

Company B

Sales Dollars and Units	Fixed Cost	Variable Cost	Total Cost	Pretax Profit or Loss
300,000	$300,000	90,000	390,000	(90,000)
350,000	300,000	105,000	405,000	(55,000)
400,000	300,000	120,000	420,000	(20,000)
450,000	300,000	135,000	435,000	15,000
500,000	300,000	150,000	450,000	50,000
550,000	300,000	165,000	465,000	85,000

Each table shows results at six sales levels. Charts representing results at all sales levels can be prepared from the tables. These provide better visual presentations of operating leverage than the tables. These are shown in Figure 5-4.

The breakeven point is reached when total sales revenue exactly equals the total of fixed and variable costs. Sales above that level

Figure 5-4

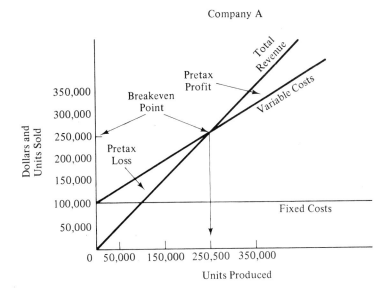

Company A

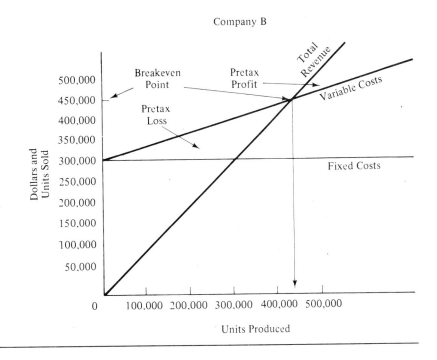

Company B

produce profits and below that level create losses. The breakeven point formula is:

$$\text{Breakeven Point} = \frac{\text{Fixed Costs}}{\text{Unit Price} - \text{Variable Cost per Unit}}$$

For Company A:

$$\text{Breakeven Point} = \frac{\$100,000}{\$1.00 - .60} = 250,000 \text{ units}$$

For Company B:

$$\text{Breakeven Point} = \frac{\$300,000}{\$1.00 - .30} = 428,571 \text{ units}$$

INTERPRETING OPERATING LEVERAGE

Calculating the breakeven point helps the analyst predict profits and losses at various levels of sales as well as the sales volume required to break even. Of perhaps more importance, however, is the information conveyed by the shape of the profit and loss wedges in each chart. The shape of these wedges shows the impact of operating leverage and suggests the risk imposed by a high level of fixed costs.

Company A (see Figures 5-3 and 5-4) is in an industry with low fixed costs and high variable costs. The investment required for plant and equipment is relatively small, but the direct labor cost per unit (for example) is high. Profits climb slowly after the breakeven point is reached. Conversely, losses grow moderately as sales drop below the breakeven point.

Company B (see Figures 5-3 and 5-4) is in a high fixed cost industry. Its profits increase sharply after the breakeven point is reached, but losses grow rapidly as well if sales fall below the breakeven point.

The tendency for losses to expand rapidly as sales decline is the result of a high degree of operating leverage. Operating leverage produces risk as a result of the fixed costs of production just as financial leverage produces risk as a result of the fixed interest cost of debt. The commercial lending officer should be cognizant of the potentially rapid decline in profitability of borrowers with high fixed costs.

SPREADING FINANCIAL STATEMENTS

An important tool used by commercial lenders in statement analysis is the spread sheet. A sample spread sheet is shown in Figure 5-5. It should be prepared as part of the initial evaluation process and

Figure 5-5. Sample Spread Sheet

COMPANY NAME_____ ADDRESS _____

ASSETS	19___	%	19___	%	19___	%	19___	%	19___	%
Cash										
Notes Receivable										
Accts. Rec.										
Inventory										
Stocks & Bonds										
Current Assets										
Land—Bldgs.(Net)										
Mche.Fur.&Fix.Equipt.(Net)										
TOTAL ASSETS										
LIABILITIES										
Notes Payable (Banks)										
Notes Payable (Trade)										
Accts. Pay										
Miscellaneous Accruals										
Current Liabilities										
Mortgages										
Total Debts										
Owner's Equity										
Surplus & Un. Profits										
TOTAL LIAB. & EQUITY										
Sales										
Cost of Sales										
Gross Profit										
Selling Exp.										
Gen'l & Admin. Exp.										
Net Profits Bef. Tax										
Net Profits										
Net Cash Generated										
Dividends Paid										

extended each time a new set of statements is received once a lending relationship has been established. Because the spread sheet facilitates tracking developments within the company, its greatest value derives from its use in follow-up procedures after the loan is made.

The balance sheet and income statement values are entered on the spread sheet in dollar amounts, and for larger companies, may be rounded to the nearest $100 or $1,000. In the percent column each asset should be expressed as a percentage of total assets, each liability or net worth item as a percentage of total liabilities and net worth. Each income statement value should be shown as a percentage of sales. The spread sheet may also include a section for loan history, a list of pertinent ratios which should be calculated or any other pertinent information.

The spread sheet focuses on internal comparisons over time. It may help raise such questions as "why did cost of goods sold suddenly rise from 75 percent to 80 percent of sales?" Further analysis may provide the reasons. If not, it may be necessary to meet with the customer. And very importantly, completing the spread sheet may give warning signs early enough to avoid repayment problems.

FINANCIAL PROJECTIONS

Financial statements are historical documents. The analysis discussed so far in this chapter has dealt with methods of processing the historical values from statements to improve the assessment of possible future outcomes. However, the financial information required from the prospective or actual commercial borrower should not be limited to historical statements. The commercial lender should require financial projections in some form.

The borrower may feel that the future is too uncertain to make meaningful projections. However, it should be stressed that projecting financial values is part of the overall planning process so essential to business success. Making well thought out financial projections is a valuable disciplinary effort for the borrowing firm as well as being of help to the lender in making loan decisions.

Reluctance to make financial projections should not be a problem with larger firms, though small companies often find this a major challenge. Big corporations often have planning departments that make extensive projections into the future based on various assumptions about market conditions, the economy, new product development or virtually any development which could affect the company.

BUDGETS

A budget is a projection of a certain facet of a firm's activities. A budget may be prepared for virtually any activity where outcomes can have an important influence on the firm. For example, a raw materials budget, a selling expense budget and a production budget might be prepared. However, the commercial lending officer will usually be most interested in the cash budget.

Cash Budget

All business borrowers, no matter how small the company, should prepare cash budgets. It shows how the company expects cash to be provided in future periods and where it expects it to be expended. A sample cash budget is shown in Figure 5-6.

Figure 5-6. Cash Budget

XYZ Company
Cash Budget, January 198A

Receipts	
Cash Sales	$ 500
Collection of Accounts Receivable	800
Interest on Securities	200
Property Rental Income	200
Total Receipts	$ 1,700
Disbursements	
Acccounts Payable	$ 900
Federal and State Taxes	200
Payroll Expense	400
Mortgage Payment	200
Dividends to Stockholders	200
Total Disbursements	$ 1,900
Receipts less Disbursements	$ (200)
Add Beginning Cash Balance	$ 500
Ending Cash Balance	$ 300

The cash budget in Figure 5-6 is for one month. In practice, the cash budget will be prepared for each month for at least one year in advance. Preparing the budget allows a company to plan well in advance for any cash shortage by arranging for a loan or taking other steps. The cash budget is helpful to the lending institution as an aid to understanding the firm's needs and assessing its ability to meet loan repayments.

PRO FORMA STATEMENTS

While a budget is a projection of a single aspect of a firm, pro forma income statements and balance sheets are projections of the firm's entire operations and financial condition at some future date. If pro forma statements are based on realistic assumptions (and this is crucial) and good planning processes, their use can be an aid in commercial lending situations.

The first step in preparing the pro forma income statement is to estimate sales for the period being considered. With a projection of sales revenue which is reasonable in light of economic conditions, competition and other considerations, the cost of goods sold and other expenses can be estimated with reasonable accuracy. These should be realistic based on past experience. For example, if general and administrative expense was $200,000 last year, a projection of $100,000 might be unrealistic. Once the net income estimate is computed and the assumed payout to owners is deducted, the amount remaining is the estimated increase in retained earnings.

The pro forma balance sheet incorporates the estimated increase in retained earnings as well as any other anticipated increases or decreases in liability or owner's equity accounts. Known or expected changes in assets must be reflected. The expected levels of inventory and accounts receivable must be consistent with the results projected in the pro forma income statement. Obviously, any major expansion of assets must be offset by the increase in the expected sources of financing shown on the right side of the balance sheet—owner's equity or short- or long-term debt.

SUMMARY

The financial statements of business customers provide important information that is essential to the lending process and follow-up procedures after a loan is made. The analysis of financial statements can take several forms so it is necessary to learn to apply only those methods which produce the desired answers.

Statement analysis is efficient in that much information can be generated in a short period of time if analysis is based on current, comprehensive statements. However, total reliance on statement analysis should not be the rule. Its greatest value is in identifying areas that require further analysis.

Ratio analysis is a basic form of financial statement analysis. Normally ratios are calculated to help give a better understanding of a firm's liquidity, asset management effectiveness, riskiness due to financial leverage and profitability.

Interpreting financial ratios usually includes comparison with average ratios of other firms in the same industry. In addition, a ratio can be compared with the same ratio in prior periods to see if a trend is developing which could have undesirable consequences. Relating a firm's asset turnover ratio to its net margin can be important in assessing its ability to improve profitability.

Breakeven analysis is an important analytical method based on a firm's fixed production costs. Fixed costs impose operating leverage, and the greater the operating leverage the more rapidly profits rise or fall as revenues rise above or fall below the breakeven point. The breakeven point is that level of sales which produces revenue equal to total costs.

Financial statement spreading is a method of displaying the information in financial statements to facilitate comparison of the firm's condition from one period to the next. Financial projections include preparation of cash budgets and pro forma financial statements.

CHAPTER QUESTIONS

1. Why should the financial analyst calculate the acid test ratio as well as the current ratio in evaluating a firm's liquidity?
2. How does the inventory turnover ratio help judge a firm's management effectiveness?
3. Why is it important to calculate financial leverage ratios? Profitability ratios?
4. Once ratios are calculated, why is it important to compare them to industry averages or standards?
5. What is the relationship between net margin and asset turnover?
6. Why would the breakeven point of a company be important in considering its application for a loan?
7. What is the purpose of pro forma financial statements?

6

Commercial
Lending Policy

OBJECTIVES

After reading Chapter 6, you should be able to:

- Explain the purpose of commercial lending policy;
- Give examples of the important determinants of a commercial lending policy;
- Discuss small business as an area of commercial lending opportunity;
- Describe the role and changing meaning of the prime rate;
- List at least three of the items which might be included in a detailed policy covering accounts receivable lending.

Once the management of a financial institution has made the decision to enter the field of commercial lending, the next step is to prepare a written commercial lending policy. The process of preparing a comprehensive, written policy will bring forth many of the questions that should be answered before the commercial lending program is initiated. Answering these questions in the policy-writing stage may avoid many expensive, time consuming problems later on. The purpose of this chapter is to identify considerations in the policy-writing process and describe some possible results of that effort.

PURPOSE OF THE COMMERCIAL LENDING POLICY

A policy is a guide to action. The policies of an institution provide the guidelines for operating management and other employees to conduct their day-by-day activities. To be effective, it is important for policy to strike a balance. It should not be so extensive and detailed that it stifles all the initiative and judgment of individual employees, yet it should be sufficiently precise and comprehensive to provide guidelines for employees and assure consistency in their actions.

The purposes of commercial lending policy are to: 1) provide guidelines for those employees involved in the commercial lending function; 2) produce loans that contribute to profitability of the organization and 3) limit the risk to which depositors' funds are exposed in the commercial lending process. This chapter is concerned primarily with the first two purposes. Much of the discussion of financial analysis in Chapter 5 was concerned with identifying risk; categories of risk were defined in Chapter 2. Risk will be included as a factor in pricing loans which is discussed later in this chapter.

DIRECTORS' ROLE IN COMMERCIAL LOAN POLICY

The board of directors is responsible for establishing policy and operating personnel apply the policy. Normally board members do not actually write the policies, but they review and accept or reject policy proposals presented by operating officers. In the case of commercial lending policy, however, many boards may find it desirable to involve one or more of the board members in the initial formulation and writing of proposed policies.

This is suggested because, first, many boards include members of the business community who are familiar with various forms of commercial credit (likely having been borrowers themselves). Few, if any, employees of organizations just entering commercial lending will have had any exposure to this type of lending. Second, the risks, required analysis, pricing considerations and many other elements of commercial lending are different from real estate and consumer lending. These elements should be introduced gradually to the board and digested slowly during the policy-writing process. This process will be facilitated if one or more board members is involved in the nuts and bolts activity of putting together policy recommendations and keeping the board apprised of progress.

COORDINATION WITH OTHER ACTIVITIES

Commercial lending policy must assure that commercial lending activity complements other activities of the financial institution. This point has both internal and external implications. Internally, the allocation of personnel, resources and funds for lending purposes to the commercial lending function should be commensurate with its potential contribution within regulatory limitations.

The focus of policy in terms of external considerations should be to make sure that entry into commercial lending does not have a negative effect on other aspects of the business. It should fit in, in the eyes of the customers, with the image the organization has developed in the community. For example, if the financial institution seems to be eagerly seeking business loans while turning away mortgage or consumer loan applications, the result may be to produce an image of inconsistency.

OTHER BENEFITS OF A WRITTEN POLICY

Preparation of written policy, including commercial lending policy, is helpful to management in adapting to changing conditions, revising existing objectives and establishing new objectives. Policy should be sufficiently flexible to adapt to some change, but there should be no hesitation to revise policy as new conditions begin to emerge.

Good policy tends to push decision making down to lower levels of authority, thus helping develop future senior management. The employees generally know what actions to take if policy is effective; thus it avoids the bottleneck problem that exists when all decision making is concentrated in one or two senior people. In other words, the policy helps in delegation of authority. One mark of a well-managed organization is a high degree of delegated authority.

Good policy is also an excellent training device for new employees and seasoned employees new to an activity such as commercial lending.

This is particularly so if policy is written with explanations given for required procedures.

ELEMENTS OF A COMMERCIAL LENDING POLICY

Each financial institution has its own unique characteristics, so the commercial lending policy suitable to one may not fit another. The policy that fits a large organization may be too extensive for a small one. Geographic differences, the nature of competition, management philosophies and many other influences will result in the formation of commercial lending policy which is significantly different from one institution to another. Many considerations will be common to most operations, however, and it is the purpose of this section to identify the most important of those common elements.

BUSINESS OPPORTUNITIES

Prior to making the decision to enter the field of commercial lending, an institution will have concluded that sufficient lending opportunities exist in its market area to justify its entry. This may have been accomplished by discussions with people from the business community, analysis of population trends and other developments in the market area, use of professional marketing surveys or a combination of methods. The results of this feasibility study should be brought into the policy-writing process to be used in defining the categories of business lending that will be emphasized. At least in the early years of the commercial lending activity most financial institutions probably will want to limit the range of their activity to those areas of lending that seem to offer the best opportunity for success.

Credit Needs of the Community

The credit needs of businesses in a trade area will have been indicated in the feasibility study and this will help determine the types of loans that should be emphasized. These should be set forth in the policy. It may be that emphasis will be placed on one or more classes of loans, such as inventory financing. The emphasis may be on one or more particular industries that are important in the trade area.

Opportunity may be obvious if the credit needs of certain business groups are not being met. More often, opportunity will be found in those areas of business where credit needs are met to a limited degree, resulting in dissatisfaction of borrowers. This may be particularly true of small businesses.

Credit Problems of Small Business

The owners of small firms frequently do not feel they have attractive alternatives for their credit needs. They often feel they are the first to be denied credit during recession or periods of tight money. They believe that lenders favor large companies at such times because they do not want the large companies to take their business elsewhere.

If some small firms feel their credit needs are met with some indifference, this feeling may be enhanced by what they consider unreasonably high rates of interest when credit is available. Other concerns often involve service. Are they limited in their contact with lenders to junior personnel who cannot make decisions? Does it take an unjustifiable period of time to get responses to their applications?

Many institutions with little or no experience may choose to limit their lending to small firms. This may be most suitable for smaller institutions or those which decide to limit their commercial lending to a small part of the total lending activity. It may be that small businesses will provide all the commercial lending opportunities needed.[1]

LOAN STANDARDS

The generally high quality standard of loans that typically have already been made should be understood by employees without reference to policy. The funds loaned by the financial intermediary belong to depositors and must not be subjected to undue risk. It is appropriate, however, that policy include a brief statement conveying the high quality standards of the intermediary.

Quality in a commercial loan derives from the financial strength of the firm, its business prospects and capability of management. These are judged in the credit analysis process after an application is taken. Wasted effort may be avoided, however, if policy defines certain types of loans which normally will not comply with the institution's standards. Where the potential customer's interest in such a loan is expressed in the initial interview, it should not be necessary even to accept an application. The list in Figure 6-1 suggests some of the types of loans which an intermediary may decide to exclude.

---

[1] Ross B. Kenzie, "A Savings Banker Looks at Commercial Lending," The *Journal of Commercial Bank Lending*, April 1981, p. 34.

Figure 6-1. Loans that May Be Considered Unacceptable

1. Loans to anyone of questionable integrity.

2. Loans to new business or new owners of an existing business with limited management experience where repayment depends on profitable operation of the firm.

3. Loans based on closely held common stock for which there is no ready market.

4. Loans to weak borrowers based on the endorsement of a strong guarantor.

5. Loans to engage in inventory speculation.

6. Loans of a short-term nature to finance long-term assets.

7. Loans where the source of repayment is to be derived from future loans or sales of stock.

8. Loans of a long-term nature which are not amortized.

9. Loans for construction purposes when there is no commitment for permanent financing.

MATURITY GUIDELINES

Term loans and other forms of intermediate-term business loans are subject to the interest rate risk defined in Chapter 2. Primarily, the risk is that after a loan is made interest rates may rise so that the cost of funds is higher than the rate on the loan. This is a situation all too familiar to many financial institutions because of the rising interest rates of the late 1970s and early 1980s which created a negative spread between cost of funds and the yield on loan portfolios. There may be a tendency to want to limit commercial loan maturities to short-term only. However, floating rates can largely remove the interest rate risk from longer-term loans.

There is an additional risk factor associated with a firm's future profitability relative to its ability to repay short-term, self-liquidating loans. This may encourage some intermediaries to limit their lending to only short-term loans. However, as pointed out in Chapter 4, many businesses have a significant need for longer-term credit. Thus, an institution may not have the opportunity to make short-term loans to many businesses if it cannot provide some longer-term credit as well.

An appropriate maturity policy might be one that establishes a ceiling on the proportion, say 10 or 20 percent, of the commercial loan portfolio that will consist of loans maturing in over one year. This would be a means to limit and control the risk exposure from

longer-term credit while still making such loans available to deserving businesses.

ORGANIZATION'S SIZE AND STRUCTURE

A small organization will probably require a less extensive policy than a large operation for at least three reasons. First, the smaller organization will probably stress smaller, less complicated loans. Second, it will probably lend to fewer different types of businesses. Third, with fewer people involved in the activity, more decisions are made at higher levels of management so fewer guidelines are needed. Even though policy may not be lengthy, it should be designed with care.

A large organization with a system of branches may require an extensive, detailed policy. An organization with branches may centralize the analysis and decision making involved in commercial lending in its head office. Branch personnel, who may have other areas of responsibility as well, may never develop extensive expertise in commercial lending. Thus, policy may be required to guide the branch personnel through the many steps required to provide good service to branch commercial customers.

DELEGATION OF AUTHORITY

Policy should spell out the structure of the commercial lending function. The size, management positions and organization of the commercial lending department (or group) should be defined. The loan limits of each officer, or level of officers, should be specified as well as the types of loans to which the limits apply. For example, limits might be higher for loans made to existing customers than to new ones, or for an inventory loan than for a term loan.

The committee structure applicable to the commercial lending function should be defined and the members specified. Frequency of meetings and procedures for reviewing loan applications and other business should be described.

How much lending authority to delegate to individual officers will depend on many considerations, including management philosophy. Also of importance is the experience and ability of commercial lending personnel. If it is deemed appropriate to develop a meaningful level of commercial loan business in a short time, one or more experienced officers may be hired to help bring this about. If this is the case, the organization may want to delegate a significant level of lending authority to such people. If a gradual development process is contemplated, delegation of authority might be very limited while personnel, management and the board of directors gain experience.

Value of Good Service

If delegation of individual authority is quite limited, management must take care to see that the loan approval (or rejection) process is fast. One complaint, particularly by many small businesses, is that lenders take excessive amounts of time to respond as applications go through managers and committees. One area of opportunity for new commercial lenders is to provide fast, high-quality service. If individual employees have the authority to give answers without waiting for various committees to meet, the potential for good services in a short time is enhanced. Such employees should, of course, be well-trained and experienced.

COMMITMENTS

Loan commitments of various forms were defined in Chapters 3 and 4. Commercial loan policy should set forth the types of commitments which the association will grant, the borrower qualifications necessary for such commitments and methods of controlling the level of commitments. Applicable fees for commitments and any compensating balance requirements should be spelled out.

Loan commitments provide a desirable approach to the commercial lending process. A line of credit agreement, for example, can be an aid to both the customer and the lender in projecting forthcoming activity. However, the lender must maintain control on the volume of commitments outstanding. A commitment means the intermediary will have funds available when the business wants them, and if the lender was too generous in granting commitments in prior months, it may find suddenly that its liquidity is strained to provide the funds. Or, the lender may experience expansion of its commercial loan portfolio just as poor economic conditions would call for the opposite, because businesses are taking down their commitments.

PROBLEM LOANS

As soon as a loan payment is overdue, it should appear on a report distributed to management. An immediate and continuing effort should be made to correct the delinquency or otherwise make sure the position of the lender is protected. The steps to be taken should be spelled out in policy and strictly adhered to. Working with problem loans will be discussed in Chapter 10.

It is vital that policy and/or senior management decisions intervene as soon as a loan is delinquent because suddenly the lender is "at risk" to a much greater degree than previously recognized. Hopefully the relationship between lending officers and customers is positive and even when the customer is under some financial duress, the lending officer will have been notified. However, policy must cover any problem situation. Loan officers in some cases may feel responsible for the problem so they seek to work out problems on their own. As a result, they may be led to make poor decisions. This is less likely to happen if the situation is covered by policy.

PRICING COMMERCIAL LOANS

All aspects of the commercial lending process may be carried out to perfection, but if the interest rate charged the customer is too low, then the entire process has failed. Conversely, if rates quoted are too high, the customer probably will go elsewhere to borrow no matter how positive the other features of the loan program. The commercial lending policy should spell out the method of establishing interest rates to assure as nearly as possible that the borrower is treated fairly while the lender earns a fair return.

This does not mean policy should spell out specific rates. Rather policy should describe the method by which a rate is computed so the loan officer can make the computation. A modest degree of latitude should be provided the loan officer in setting the rate, but two officers working with identical loan applications should arrive at rates nearly if not exactly equal. Prior to discussing the ingredients of loan pricing, consideration will be given to the role of the prime rate.

ROLE OF THE PRIME RATE

The *prime rate* has long been defined as the rate commercial banks charge their most creditworthy business borrowers. Big money-center banks usually take the lead in changing the prime and other banks follow along, so the prime is equal, or nearly so, at most banks most of the time. If one bank tried to operate with a significantly higher prime, its business lending would decline sharply. If it set its prime significantly below other banks, it would be inundated with loan requests. So even though banks are free, in theory, to set their own prime, they are virtually locked in to what is happening in the entire banking industry.

Changing Meaning of the Prime

The prime rate has lost some of its meaning in recent years. When it was originated during the depression of the 1930s, it was the product of the desire of several large banks to avoid price competition. These banks agreed they would not make business loans at less than 1-1/2 percent. As time went by the prime became much more subject to competitive influences, with banks no longer colluding to set the rate.[2]

The result continued to appear much the same as if the rate were set through collusion, however, since it was the same at most banks most of the time and apparently set as high as the traffic would bear. During the late 1960s the prime came under criticism, particularly from some members of Congress, because it appeared to be the result of collusion and partly the cause of (at that time) high interest rates.

First National City Bank in New York took a step in 1971 to stave off such criticism by allowing its rate to be determined by free market rates. Presumably, if its prime was the result of other rates, it could not be considered a cause of interest rate levels. The bank determined that its prime would be one half percent above the rate on dealer placed 90-day commercial paper, to be reviewed and, if necessary, adjusted weekly. Other banks from time to time adopted some form of this formula approach to setting the prime, but many discarded the approach after criticism moderated. However, because changes had become frequent and variances were common, the meaning of the prime as the lowest rate the banking system offered business borrowers had started to diminish.

Two developments in recent years have tended to produce a higher prime. First, more and more banks have reduced emphasis on compensating balances to provide part of the return on business loans. This means they charge higher stated rates and, consequently, maintain a higher prime than if the compensating balance requirement was as extensive as in the past.

Second, with so many outstanding floating-rate loans based on the prime, banks are reluctant to reduce it because of the loss of revenue which would result.[3] One's first reaction to this point might be that reluctance to lower the prime must cause a great many potential business borrowers to seek credit from sources other than banks. To a degree this is true. The commercial paper market, for example, has

---

[2] Today, collusion to set interest rates would be a violation of anti-trust laws.

[3] Randall C. Merris, "Business Loans at Large Commercial Banks: Policies and Practices," *Economic Perspectives*, November/December 1979, pp. 15-23. Federal Reserve Bank of Chicago.

expanded dramatically in recent years. However, banks have found a way to prevent loss of business of large, financially strong firms. They simply lend at rates below the prime.[4] This activity is, more than any other development, depleting the meaning of the prime.

IS THE PRIME NECESSARY?

Although the prime has lost some of its significance, it remains the commercial lending benchmark in the U.S. Commercial borrowers are oriented to the concept of a prime rate. Floating rates, which are now common to commercial lending, are pegged to each lender's prime. Small and medium-sized banks often follow the lead of a specific large bank operating in or near their area, changing when the large bank does and adopting the same rate. Other financial intermediaries may also follow this example. This procedure can save a significant amount of time and deliberation.

The prime is merely the beginning point when determining the actual rates charged customers, and there are other features to consider as well. Even if various financial intermediaries adopt the prime prevailing in the banking industry, each can set its own effective loan rates because:

1. It will determine which of its borrowers are charged the prime and how much above the prime the others are charged.
2. It will decide whether compensating balances are required and, if so, their extent.
3. It will set the loan to value for collateralized loans, which loans can be made without collateral and other factors which influence quality in a loan.
4. It will decide if interest rate ceilings will be placed on floating rate loans, thus removing some of the earnings potential as well as some of the interest-rate risk from the borrower.

Commercial loan policy should specify how to compute loan rates. The two components of loan rates are the cost of funds and the spread between cost of funds and the rate charged the borrower.

COST OF FUNDS

The cost of funds is expressed as a percentage rate. It consists almost entirely of interest paid on deposits, although interest on Federal

---

[4] "Borrowing at Less Than the Prime Rate," *Dun's Business Month*, September 1981, pp. 91-93.

Reserve and Federal Home Loan Bank advances and on other borrowed funds is included.

Marginal Cost

The cost of funds computed in this manner is the average rate applicable to all funds used. An intermediary may prefer to use the marginal (incremental) cost of funds. For example, the average cost of funds might be 12 percent, but if interest rates were in a rising trend so that last month the average cost of new deposits was 13 percent, then the lender might consider 13 percent as the appropriate cost of funds. This would help protect the profitability of the commercial lending activity during a period of rising rates.

At times the difference between average cost and marginal cost may be substantial. To illustrate this point a hypothetical example will be used. The example is based on a very simple financial institution that has only two forms of deposits: passbook savings and time certificates. At time A its passbook accounts are paying 5 percent and its certificates 10 percent. Each form of deposit comprises half the total, so:

<u>Time A</u>

Passbook accounts @ 5% x 1/2	= 2.5%
Time CDs @ 10% x 1/2	= 5.0
Average cost of funds	= 7.5%

By the next point in time, time B, after a sharp rise in interest rates, the financial institution still has half of its deposits in passbook savings and the total balance has not changed. The total amount in certificates also has not changed, but of the deposit total only 30 percent remains in 10 percent certificates and 20 percent is in 15 percent certificates. This is because maturing 10 percent certificates were renewed at 15 percent, so:

<u>Time B</u>

Passbook accounts @ 5% x 1/2	= 2.5%
Time CDs @ 10% x 3/10	= 3.0
Time CDs @ 15% x 2/10	= 3.0
Average cost of funds	= 8.5%

Average cost rose from 7.5 percent to 8.5 percent from time A to time B. Marginal cost, however, should be viewed as 15 percent at time B, because that was the cost to the institution for the latest funds acquired. If loan rates are set considering only the average cost, the financial institution could be in the position of charging, say, 11 or 12 percent on loans made with money which costs 15 percent.

Effect of Compensating Balances

The cost of the funds used by the borrower (plus the appropriate spread) must be recovered. If compensating balances are required, however, the funds used by the borrower will be less than the amount of the loan.

For example, if a borrower has drawn $100,000 under a line of credit agreement, but has $20,000 on deposit as a result of a compensating balance requirement, then obviously the borrower is not getting the use of $100,000. However, if the lender bases recovery of its cost of funds on $80,000 it will be shortchanging itself. Why? Because it must maintain part of the $20,000 as reserves on which it earns nothing. If the reserve requirement on the $20,000 were 15 percent, then $3,000 would be a nonearning reserve.

SPREAD

The spread added to the cost of funds to determine the rate charged the borrower must be sufficient to: 1) cover all costs of making and servicing the loan; 2) cover the pro rata allocation of overhead; 3) allow for the risk factor applicable to the loan; 4) provide a fair profit. Since there is no perfect method of determining any of these, many assumptions and compromises will go into determining an appropriate spread. The experienced judgment of the lending officer also will be an ingredient.

The risk factor reflects the chance that the borrower may not repay all or part of the loan. The less creditworthy the borrower, the higher the rate which should be required. Also, some types of loans are inherently riskier than others and thus should carry the highest rates. No matter how well managed a commercial lending program may be, there will be losses from time to time. Theoretically, over time, the portion of the spread applicable to risk should offset those losses.

Just what comprises a fair profit will rest on management's judgment. What is considered fair may change from time to time as economic conditions change, interest rates rise and fall, and competition intensifies or recedes.

POLICIES FOR SPECIFIC LOAN CATEGORIES

Many of the general considerations involved in forming a commercial lending policy have been discussed to this point. The lender will also want to consider the extent to which a separate policy is written for each type of loan it expects to make. These specific policies might be quite brief, or, if most of the employees involved in commercial lending have limited experience, a policy might be quite detailed, including explanations.

Figure 6-2 offers an example of a detailed policy pertaining to accounts receivable lending. It should be stressed that this example is limited in that it does not include specifications for follow-up and servicing after a loan is made. Also, it almost certainly omits many elements which many lenders would consider necessary. It should, however, suggest the nature of a detailed loan policy.

Figure 6-2. Example of Detailed Policy Covering Loans Secured by Accounts Receivable

Loan Policy X-XX	Loans Secured by Accounts Receivable

Loans secured by accounts receivable should be for the purpose of financing current assets. The loans should not finance long-term assets. The borrowing company should be looking toward replacing debt secured by accounts receivable with permanent capital (additional owner's equity or long-term debt) after some reasonable period. It is preferable that the firm clean up its accounts receivable loan at least once a year and remain out of debt to this institution for at least 60 days.

Rapidly growing firms in particular can benefit from accounts receivable financing because their receivables and inventory expand more rapidly than their ability to finance these assets. Dependency on receivables financing should not become excessive, however, and at some point the investment in permanent current assets must be provided by long-term sources.

During the initial discussion with the customer, use of this institution's charge card to replace the customer's present credit-granting system should be explored. If accounts are small, as in the case of many retail-type firms, use of our charge card might be advantageous. The firm eliminates the cost of its credit department, frees the funds invested in receivables and no longer has collection problems.

Preferred receivables from the standpoint of granting credit are those of well-established firms with high standards for granting credit to customers. Individually, the receivables should be for reasonable amounts, and payment records should be supplied for each customer. Non-notification of the borrower's customers is preferred by this institution and by borrowing firms. If it appears notification is required, then making the loan at all is called into question.

Figure 6-2 (Continued)

Points of Evaluation. The loan officer should be sure that the following are acceptable and/or well understood:

A. The borrower's cash flow.
B. The borrower's financial projections (usually cash budgets and pro forma financial statements).
C. Financial strength of the borrower's customers.
D. Any concentrations of sales to particular customers (financial information should be obtained on any such customers).
E. What discounts and terms does borrower provide its customers?
F. What is borrower's experience with returns and refunds?
G. What are borrower's collection policies?
H. What are borrower's billing procedures?
I. Are any receivables for services not yet performed?
J. Assure that proceeds will not be used to finance fixed assets or provide funds for withdrawals by owners.
K. Specify to the borrower that an aging schedule for accounts receivable is to be provided monthly.

Documents and Other Requirements. The loan officer must assure that the following are obtained and are in order:

A. Loan application.
B. Current financial statements.
C. Financial statements for prior two years.
D. Dun and Bradstreet report.
E. Credit report.
F. Corporate or partnership borrowing resolution.
G. Promissory note.
H. Security agreement.
I. Uniform Commercial Code financing statement.
J. Current aging schedule.

Loan Specifications. Accounts receivable loans shall be on a demand basis. Proceeds up to 75 percent of the face value of receivables less than 30 days past due may be advanced. Interest is to be billed and paid monthly.

SUMMARY

The preparation of a written policy should be the first step after the decision is made to enter the field of commercial lending. The purposes of the commercial lending policy are to: 1) provide guidelines for employees involved in commercial lending; 2) produce loans which contribute to profitability and 3) limit the risk resulting from commercial loans made.

The basic elements which go into forming the commercial lending policy include legal limitations, business opportunities, desired loan standards, maturity considerations, size and structure of the lending institution, methods of delegation of authority, treatment of loan commitments and problem loans. Perhaps the most important single consideration in forming policy is the method of pricing loans. Rates charged must return to the lender its cost of funds plus a spread which covers other costs, allows for the risk of the loan and provides a reasonable profit.

In addition to policies covering general considerations, policies covering each specific class of loan may be desired. These may be very brief, covering only a few essential points, or they may be comprehensive and detailed.

CHAPTER QUESTIONS

1. Why should a commercial lending policy set minimum quality standards for loans to be made?

2. Why is it important that policy set forth the manner of handling loan commitments?

3. How has the importance of the prime rate diminished in recent years?

4. Should a nonbank financial intermediary employ the prime rate prevailing in the commercial banking industry in pricing its commercial loans?

5. Cite an advantage and a disadvantage of requiring compensating balances.

7

Developing Commercial Lending Opportunities

OBJECTIVES

After reading Chapter 7, you should be able to:

- Describe the nature of commercial loan marketing;
- Define the national market and local market for commercial loans;
- List at least five complaints given by business borrowers concerning their credit arrangements;
- List at least five sources of potential business customers;
- Explain the procedure which should be followed in a call program.

Entering the field of commercial lending means that a lending institution will have a broader line of products and services to offer the community. This broader line will require an expansion of the marketing function. The marketing of commercial loans is only a part of each organization's overall marketing strategy. However, several aspects of commercial lending are unique and will require separate consideration in order to integrate commercial lending into the overall marketing strategy. This chapter examines some of the important concepts to consider in developing commercial lending opportunities.

MARKETING COMMERCIAL LOANS

Marketing can be viewed as being synonomous with selling. Selling is an important part—but only a part—of the marketing process. Marketing can be defined as follows:

Financial institution marketing is a management function. Its purpose is to identify and provide, at a profit, financially related services which customers want and need. The primary functions of financial institution marketing include: marketing research, planning, financial services development, financial services delivery systems, pricing recommendations, advertising, public relations, sales and special promotions and sales training.[1]

The customers of a commercial lending service are, of course, the business firms to which loans are made. Although each lending institution has one or more officers responsible for the overall coordination of the marketing effort, marketing is, to some degree, the responsibility of every employee.

IMPORTANCE OF MARKETING

The importance of marketing cannot be overemphasized. Anyone who reads the newspaper or hears and sees news programs knows that the financial institutions business is undergoing change. To progress and survive during this period, financial intermediaries must emphasize marketing programs that meet the definition of marketing given above. These institutions must identify viable markets, develop new and

---

[1] The Institute of Financial Education, *Marketing for Financial Institutions* (Chicago, IL: The Institute of Financial Education, 1982), pp. 5-6.

beneficial products and services, and communicate with customers and potential customers in the most effective way possible.

Even though commercial lending will be a new activity to many financial institutions and their employees, they should remember that the market for commercial loans is large. If the program is well supported by a strong marketing effort, the commercial lending function can become an important and beneficial activity for many lenders.

NATURE OF COMMERCIAL LOAN MARKETING

The nature of commercial loan marketing is individualistic. Although policy will set down types of loans to be pursued and procedures to be followed, each business has unique features that will make each lending situation different. Obtaining the credit business of a given firm requires understanding its unique features.

Because each situation is different, a personal relationship must be developed between the owner or manager of a small firm and one or more of the lender's employees in order to successfully market the commercial lending product. This relationship should be professional in nature and not one of the hard-sell variety.

NEED FOR MARKETING RESEARCH

The decision to make commercial loans will be based on a number of factors. One of the most important of these should be the results of a market study that indicate that there is a sufficient level of potential business in the market area to justify entry into commercial lending. The study may be formal and extensive, utilizing professional researchers and including surveys, population studies and/or any number of methods of researching the market. Or, it may be informal and brief, consisting of discussions with local business people or a process equally uncomplicated. Whatever form the study takes, such an effort is part of that element of the marketing function called marketing research. Thus, the purpose of marketing research is to identify and describe the market so that the institution can better interpret and satisfy the wants and needs of current and potential customers.[2]

Having determined that there is a sufficient number of potential customers to justify entering the field of commercial lending, the next

---

[2]*Ibid*, p. 5.

step is to determine how to make actual customers out of potential customers. This is facilitated through market segmentation. Market segmentation allows the institution to focus its marketing efforts on a specific target or group of customers. It allows a more effective marketing effort as opposed to the more costly effort aimed at a wide range of customers.[3]

IDENTIFYING THE MARKETS

Commercial loans can be viewed as having two markets: national and local. Large companies borrow in a national (and in some cases international) credit market. Such companies can borrow from the big, money-center banks, large insurance companies or finance companies, and from other institutional lenders that conduct their lending activities throughout the U.S. and, in many cases, in other countries. Large companies also raise borrowed funds in large amounts by selling their commercial paper, notes and bonds in the money and capital markets.

Small firms normally do not have access to the national market. Their borrowing opportunities usually are limited to local financial intermediaries. Although a small firm may get its business loans from a nearby branch of a large commercial bank that also lends extensively in the national credit market, the terms and conditions imposed on the small firm are the norms of the local market and not the national market. For the most part, these local norms relegate small business to a secondary status.

Large businesses have a significant degree of influence over their borrowing arrangements unless their financial position is very weak. Small businesses have little if any such influence. They cannot issue bonds, notes or commercial paper. They cannot borrow below the prime rate (see Chapter 6) as can many large firms. Small firms have few alternative sources of credit. They are limited to the local market for commercial loans.

Lending in the National Market

In the early years of commercial lending activity, the national market for commercial loans probably will not be a profitable market for most lenders new to this activity. Only the largest organizations should expect reasonable opportunities to develop lending relationships with large companies during the early years of operation. In part, this

---

[3] The Institute of Financial Education, *Savings Association Operations* (Chicago, IL: The Institute of Financial Education, 1981), pp. 226-227.

ns as large
available
low to
ften
be
eposit
es would
ne example
ince reporting
it balances every

ing in the case of large
ie street from the national
headquarters of a large corporation, or down the block from a store that is part of a national chain, and yet have no opportunity to lend to either. The financial officers of large firms communicate with lending officers in money-center banks as easily as they might contact another financial intermediary a block away.

Lending in the Local Market

There is significant evidence that many small businesses that have no borrowing alternatives except those of the local market are not well served.[5] They have too few borrowing alternatives, sometimes pay excessive rates and may receive low-quality service.

Convenience of location is important to the owners and managers of small firms. They tend to conduct their business in person, as do consumers, so they prefer to work with a lender located close by. Also, many owners and managers of small firms feel their opportunities are almost identical from one lender to another, so there is little incentive for them to leave their immediate area.

Referring once again to the definition of marketing, it seems that many financial institutions may have a significant opportunity for ". . . financially related services which customers want and need" by entering the local market for commercial loans. Of course, the first part of the definition cannot be ignored, that is, the part which refers to profitable customer relationships. One essential aspect of rendering wanted and needed services profitably is understanding the commercial customer.

---

[4] Kenneth E. Reich, "Commercial Checking Powers, if Okayed, Will Tap New Deposits," *Savings & Loan News*, December 1981, pp. 96-99.

[5] Stephen Mathis and Thomas Ulrich, "Small Business Credit: The Competitive Factor," *The Bankers Magazine*, January/February 1982, pp. 41-45.

UNDERSTANDING THE CUSTOMER

Understanding the business customer and the characteristics which make each business unique will be very important to successful lending relationships. Understanding can be enhanced in the early stages of the commercial lending program by considering some of the complaints or disappointments business people have expressed in the past regarding lenders.

COMPLAINTS EXPRESSED BY BUSINESS BORROWERS

While the following complaints or disappointments would not be expressed by all business borrowers, they emerge often enough to merit consideration. Also, while these complaints tend to come from small firms, it should not be assumed that all large companies are pleased with their results in the credit markets. However, large firms have more alternative sources of credit and they also have much more influence than small firms over their borrowing arrangements.

The following views have been expressed by business borrowers:

1. All lenders provide similar services and their requirements are alike.

2. Lenders never seem willing to be innovative. Business people understand that lenders want to avoid high-risk loans, but they wonder why lenders cannot allocate a small percentage of their loan portfolios to help new, imaginative businesses. Lenders seem to be locked into "going by the book."

3. Loan covenants are unnecessarily restrictive, placing too many limitations on borrowers while adding little protection to the lender.

4. Collateral requirements often are excessive in relation to the amounts borrowed.

5. Compensating balances are a costly and unnecessary requirement, particularly for firms that have good credit histories and long-term relationships with lenders. Higher interest rates are preferable to compensating balances. The money on deposit in the compensating balance is more valuable to most firms than to the lenders who require the balances.

6. Treatment is inconsistent by lenders, even when the relationship has been longstanding. For example, the lender was eager to make the seasonal loan last year; but this year, with tight money conditions and the demands of large corporate borrowers, the reception from the lender was poor.

Nonetheless, any institution entering the field of commercial lending may gain perspective by noting the complaints businesses express about their present lenders. This may help new lenders offer better products which benefit both borrowing firms and lending institutions.

NONCREDIT NEEDS OF SMALL FIRMS

The owners and operators of the small companies in the U.S. are, for the most part, experts at knowing the products or performing the services sold by their businesses. They are good mechanics or cooks. They know a great deal about TV sets or air conditioning units. It is those skills and that knowledge on which they base their businesses.

The owners of small businesses may not be very knowledgeable in accounting or financial projections. It was pointed out in Chapter 1 that the financial statements of small firms often are not audited by professional accountants and often are not even prepared by accountants. Many small business people do not fully understand the potential effect of economic changes. In many cases, projecting the potential of their own firm to expand its volume in its market is difficult for the owner of a small business. He or she may feel that, if the firm sold $200,000 worth of the product last month with two salespersons, then with four salespersons the firm should sell twice as much this month. He or she may not understand that it probably will be more difficult to increase sales by an additional $200,000 than it is to maintain sales at their present level.

As you can see, the operators of small firms may have difficulty projecting the increase in volume necessary to generate the funds to repay a loan. The risk produced by additional leverage may not be clear, and the liquidity pressures of short-term financing relative to long-term may not be obvious.

Lending institutions may find a great opportunity to help operators of small firms in the area of noncredit needs, providing some of the business and economic understanding that these operators do not have time to develop. Of course, providing help of this type would require a significant investment in professional time and expertise, so a return in the form of direct fees or higher interest rates should be required. Providing help in these areas of noncredit needs should lead to many high-quality long-term business relationships which are beneficial to both parties involved.

It should not be assumed that no assistance is given at present to small business to help overcome accounting or economic shortcomings. Some lenders have offered programs to help small firms do a better job of cash budgeting, planning and inventory management. Before any new lender begins making contacts with business people, it should attempt to learn what programs, if any, are offered by its competition.

IDENTIFYING POTENTIAL CUSTOMERS

An institution new to commercial lending should be able to assemble a list of potential business customers in its area with only a modest effort. Many business people will have some relationship already established with the intermediary.

There are many other sources of potential business customers. The following is a partial list of sources.

- Directors. They may be affiliated with business firms or have specific knowledge of others.
- Employees. A spouse may be employed by a potential business customer. Also, employees conduct their personal business with many firms.
- Chamber of Commerce membership list.
- New firms in the area. The Chamber of Commerce may make these known.
- City directory.
- Yellow pages.
- Local business organizations and clubs.
- Professionals (lawyers, accountants, appraisers, etc.) with whom the institution has a relationship may provide information.
- Firms whose merchandise sales have been financed through consumer loans.

BUSINESS DEVELOPMENT PROGRAMS

The purpose of a business development program is to initiate a long-term customer relationship which benefits both the business borrower and the lending institution. An organization entering the field of commercial lending must decide: 1) how large the commercial lending program will be in terms of the total dollar amount of loans outstanding and 2) how rapidly the volume of commercial loans will be brought up to the desired level. Making these decisions will help determine the type and extent of business development programs employed. Some approaches to business development may be applied only occasionally and others may be continuous. Some of the programs which may be effective are discussed below.

CALL PROGRAMS

It is unlikely that commercial lending could be conducted at all without some form of call program. Suggested guidelines for a call program appear in Figure 7-1. As much as possible, lending institutions should make personal contact with potential business customers. These personal calls should not be casual, unannounced, get-acquainted type visits. They should be planned, by appointment and with the purpose of the call made clear to the potential customer when the appointment is made. The calling officer should be prepared to explain the program and should know what information to gather about the business.

During the visit the representative should give the business person a clear picture of what can be provided, but should do so without seeming to make a commitment. The business person must understand that credit can be granted only on approval of an application accompanied by the appropriate documents.

Figure 7-1. Suggested Guidelines for a Call Program

- Place responsibility on lending officers for gaining new and maintaining existing commercial accounts.
- Develop and maintain a call list of businesses.
    - Utilize sources such as the yellow pages and the city directory.
    - Generate a mix of prospects and customers in various lines of business.
- Set goals each month for number of calls.
- Set a sales objective for each call.
- Collect company information.
    - Company name and address.
    - Owner's and manager's names.
    - Nature of business.
    - Size of business in terms of annual sales and assets.
    - Number of employees.
    - Brief history of business.
    - Outlook for business.
- Develop background information from Dun & Bradstreet report, organization files, trade checks.
- Make the contact.
    - Determine the primary decision maker.
    - State the purpose of contact.
    - Set the appointment, preferably at the place of business.
- Make the call.
    - Project a professional image.
    - Determine needs which the lender can serve.
    - Determine financial services currently received and from whom.
    - Suggest solutions to needs, utilizing lender's services.
- Complete follow-up procedures.
    - Prepare follow-up report.
    - State purpose of the call.
    - Identify what was accomplished.
    - Provide suggestions for follow-up calls.
    - Determine best method of follow-up call—phone, letter, personal visit.

The business person should be encouraged to discuss the credit needs of the business, what is currently provided by banks or other sources, and what his or her problems have been. He or she will be interested in comparing the service presently being received with those which the new organization might offer.

Follow-up to the personal visit will be a natural procedure. A thank-you letter should be sent. Very likely there will be some questions raised at the meeting which require some research, and these may be answered in the letter, or, if a beneficial relationship appears probable, a follow-up visit may be appropriate.

It is not to be expected that a good borrowing customer will be won away from the competition easily. The first call on the most credit-worthy businesses should be considered only one of many. If the representative projects a helpful, professional image and offers good, competitive service, the call program will help develop a group of credit-worthy borrowers.

The call program should be a basic business development effort and not just an activity to engage in when other work slows down. Emphasis should be placed on calling when demand for business loans is high. This is a time when many borrowers are being disappointed by the lenders they are currently doing business with, and at that time a change is most probable. Of course, when loan demand is strong, lenders will also be experiencing an influx of unsolicited customers. An effort should be made to service this business and maintain an effective call program. The unsolicited customers are likely to be the least creditworthy.

SEMINARS

The organization's involvement could be made known to businesses by sponsoring seminars for business people on topics such as cash budgeting, cash management or inventory control. A portion of each meeting could be left open for the participants to discuss topics of their choosing related to their businesses. This would help lending personnel add to their knowledge of the local business.

LETTERS OF CREDIT

The commercial letter of credit was defined in Chapter 3. When a financial intermediary issues a letter of credit to a seller of goods, it makes payment for the goods on behalf of the buyer. The financial intermediary then collects from the buyer of the goods. If appropriate arrangements have been made in advance, payment may be delayed, thus producing a loan from the financial intermediary to the firm buying the goods.

Letters of credit must be issued with caution. Not only must the buying firm meet all the lending criteria of the intermediary, but care must be taken that the goods are delivered by the seller as and when ordered. Given proper understanding, the letter of credit program can be a help in developing commercial lending business.

SMALL BUSINESS ADMINISTRATION

The Small Business Administration (SBA) loan guarantee program was discussed in Chapter 4. An organization just entering commercial lending may benefit from a meeting with the SBA office in its region. There are several reasons the SBA program may be advantageous. First, the SBA guarantees 90 percent of such loans. Second, the loans are liquid because an active secondary market exists for the guaranteed 90 percent. The lending institution can recover most of its funds, if it chooses to, while continuing the relationship with the borrower.

A third advantage to the lender includes the lending guidelines and other requirements of the SBA, so that a high level of experience is not essential on the part of the lending personnel; and, fourth, the institution can lend to new or poorly capitalized firms that would not otherwise qualify for loans. As these firms progress, many will become financially strong borrowing customers of the lending institution.

LOAN PARTICIPATIONS

Some institutions may develop a portion of their commercial loan volume by participating in loans with other lenders, such as commercial banks or insurance companies. A loan participation exists when two or more lenders share a single loan. One lender has the lead position, handling the lending process, documentation and servicing of the loan. Other institutions participate by providing part of the loaned funds and earning a pro rata share of the interest.

Some commercial banks have developed problems with loan participations because they assumed the lead bank was doing all the analysis and servicing in a satisfactory manner. Thus they paid little attention to the loans in which they participated, and were surprised when some developed problems. Any financial intermediary entering loan participations should perform credit evaluation and require documentation and financial statements just as though it was making the loan.

SUMMARY

A financial institution that decides to make commercial loans should expect to devote a significant effort to the marketing process. The businesses that may become commercial customers are unique, and thus the marketing of commercial loans entails an individualistic approach.

The small firms whose borrowing opportunities are limited to the local credit market probably will provide the majority of the lending opportunities, at least in the early years of a new lender's commercial lending experience. There is significant evidence that the lending needs of small firms are insufficiently provided for at present. Besides the shortcomings of their present borrowing arrangements, many small firms need help of a noncredit nature, such as cash planning and statement preparation.

Once the lending institution has developed a list of possible business customers, it should employ one or more business development programs. The basic approach to business development should be a call program whereby officers visit business people to discuss their credit needs and the organization's ability to meet those needs through its lending programs. Other business development programs may include seminars for business people, offering letter of credit arrangements, involvement in the SBA loan program and loan participations whereby the lead position is taken by another lender.

CHAPTER QUESTIONS

1. How is marketing different from selling?
2. Describe the nature of commercial loan marketing.
3. Why might small firms seem to offer the best commercial lending opportunities for financial intermediaries just beginning commercial lending activity?
4. List five sources of names of potential commercial customers.
5. Describe the steps of a call program.
6. How may the Small Business Administration guaranteed loan program be helpful in developing commercial lending opportunities?
7. What is a loan participation?

8

Considerations in Credit Analysis

OBJECTIVES

After reading Chapter 8, you should be able to:

- Explain the purpose of credit analysis;
- List and describe the original three C's of credit;
- List and describe at least three other categories of credit analysis;
- Cite the major features of a Dun and Bradstreet credit report;
- Describe the other major sources of credit information;
- Explain the importance of the judgment factor in credit analysis.

Credit analysis is a part of the process of determining, with as much certainty as available information can provide, whether or not a credit applicant can and will repay a loan. Credit analysis is a very broad term and includes the evaluation of virtually all information that can help in making the credit judgment. Analysis of financial statements (see Chapter 5), economic analysis (see Chapter 1), and understanding of the customer (see Chapter 7) are also part of credit analysis. This chapter discusses several important aspects of the credit analysis process that should be understood by anyone making commercial loans. These aspects can be called general considerations. Chapter 9 discusses specific considerations that may arise once an application for a loan is made.

CREDIT ANALYSIS

The process of credit analysis can be divided into three categories. These categories are character, capital and capacity, and are referred to as the three C's of credit. If a borrower is of sufficiently high *character*, it is assumed he or she will strive to repay debts no matter how difficult that becomes and even if it entails great personal sacrifice.

Capital, in the case of a business, includes not only net worth but also long-term debt. These comprise the capital structure of the firm. If the capital structure is sufficient, then the firm can add new fixed assets as needed, increase permanent current assets as required and weather a period of economic adversity. If the firm has inadequate capital, it is constantly under pressure to pay trade creditors and meet other short-term obligations. Part of the analysis of financial statements is for judging the adequacy of capital.

Capacity refers to the ability to generate funds to repay a debt. In the case of a business, the ability to generate cash flow is of primary importance. However, such considerations as the training and background of the firm's personnel can be important in judging the firm's ability to produce its product or service. Judging the quality of fixed assets, the extent of market or the nature of competition may also be considered when measuring capacity.

Recently, credit analysts have decided that three categories of analysis are insufficient to assure that evaluation of all pertinent information is completed prior to making a credit decision. Practitioners have expanded the original categories to as many as fourteen C's, though several pertain to the credit analyst rather than the borrower.[1]

---

[1] Jack R. Crigger, "An Ocean of C's," *The Journal of Commercial Bank Lending*, December 1975.

Segregating credit analysis into categories is helpful in that it gives some assurance that all important considerations will be evaluated before a credit decision is made.   It also facilitates communication within the lending organization regarding the credit analysis process. However the financial intermediary chooses to subdivide the credit analysis process as it pertains to business loans, the considerations discussed in this chapter should be examined.

CHARACTER AS IT PERTAINS TO COMMERCIAL LOANS

The concept of character includes such intangible items as honesty, decency and integrity. The credit analyst wants to judge a borrower's character in order to measure how much determination the borrower will feel to repay the debt.   Concern ranges from the possibility of outright dishonesty to a borrower's casual willingness to let the business go into bankruptcy during difficult times.

The character of most borrowers is not easy to judge. The analyst must try to obtain information about the borrower's reputation, past debt payment records and other information about how the applicant conducts his or her affairs. The problem is, of course, that the attributes of poor character often do not emerge until a period of adversity. If an applicant has never been tested by adversity, poor character traits may not be evident in any available information.

Should character be viewed the same in making business loans as in making consumer and real estate loans? Business people, particularly those working in corporations, regard the business as an entity separate from themselves. They feel the lender is a participant, almost a partner, in the business, taking its chances in order to earn interest on loaned money. With this attitude, some business people have few doubts about defaulting on a business loan if circumstances lead them to that point. A decision to allow a company to be declared bankrupt may be made just like any other business decision, i.e., in terms of its preference from a monetary standpoint. Moral compunction to repay debt may be totally lacking.

UNDERSTANDING CONDITIONS

Conditions is another credit analysis consideration. Although conditions may include legal requirements and limitations, the political climate and other considerations, it is comprised largely of economic factors. Chapter 1 stressed the importance of economic conditions in commercial lending and several of the more important economic considerations on the national level were discussed.

State of the Economy

The economy moves in a somewhat repetitive manner. This repetitive movement led to the term "business cycles." The term is somewhat misleading in that, to many, it suggests that each economic period is a duplication of a preceding period. This thinking can lead a business person to draw conclusions such as "the average recession lasts eight months. This one is eight months old so it must be almost over." Such conclusions can lead to decisions that create business disappointments.

Each economic period is unique. It has influences and characteristics unlike previous ones. However, there is a persistent tendency for the economy to follow a general pattern of recession to recovery to boom to recession. The credit analyst should understand how the businesses he or she is concerned with are likely to fare under each stage of the cycle. He or she should also stay abreast of economic information so the current state of the economy and its effect on businesses are well understood.

For example, during a boom period, which is the period of high, unsustainable economic activity at the top of the cycle, demand for products is very strong and, probably, prices have been rising sharply. These two results may have led many firms to borrow heavily to expand inventories. They wanted to avoid future price increases, and they believed a high level of sales will soon absorb the inventory.

The credit analyst, who is aware of the stage of the economy, will recognize the risk incurred by inventory expansion at such a time. If a recession begins, the business may find itself with an excessive inventory, a sharp decline in sales and continued high financing charges to carry the inventory. Moreover, the recession may have brought a reversal in prices so the inventory is suddenly worth much less than cost. Sales of the inventory, even though slow to materialize, produce losses rather than profits. Needless to say, the lending institution which was caught up in the optimism of the boom and financed the inventory buildup may find a bad loan on its books.

Local Conditions

The composition of the local economic base can be of great importance in determining the well-being of local businesses. Communities that are dependent on one industry or one company are susceptible to economic declines affecting that company or industry. For example, in an area where agriculture is the dominant industry, the local farm equipment dealers will experience sharp reductions in sales if area farmers have a poor crop year. Many farmers will decide to make old equipment last one more year. Moreover, a decline in farm income due to low prices or a poor crop may occur in a period when the balance of the economy is performing well.

The credit analyst at a lending institution in such a community must be cognizant of the potential for local business firms to suffer if the dominant local industry or company experiences decline. If the lender is a depository institution, it may also see deposits depleted rapidly as unemployed depositors withdraw funds to meet living expenses at the same time the loan portfolio is deteriorating.

The above suggests there is a danger of pyramiding risks in a one-industry or one-company locality. If a lender has loans to the companies in the dominant industry, loans to companies that are dependent on doing business with the companies in the dominant industry, and also holds significant deposits of both categories of companies, the lender's exposure is extreme. For example, during the early 1980s, localities that suffered greater economic duress than the nation in general included those communities dependent on automobile and housing related production.

INDUSTRY DIFFERENCES

By their nature, some industries are more volatile than others. In the discussion of breakeven analysis in Chapter 5, it was shown that firms with high fixed costs (high operating leverage) experience greater fluctuations in profits for a given change in sales than do firms with low fixed costs. Operating leverage usually is highest for firms in manufacturing industries because of the substantial investment required in plant and equipment.

Many industries are described as cyclical because their earnings are particularly dependent on the business cycle. The steel, paper, chemical and auto industries are examples of major industries that are considered cyclical. Major industries that are less vulnerable to the business cycle include the food, soft drink, tobacco and drug industries. On the local level the building supply store, furniture store and auto dealership may be much more subject to the influence of the business cycle than the grocery store or the corner drug store.

FORMS OF BUSINESS ORGANIZATION

The organizational form of the business applying for credit should be considered by the credit analyst. A business may be a proprietorship, a partnership or a corporation.

Proprietorships

Approximately 78 percent of the businesses in the U.S. are *proprietorships*, that is, owned by one person. The business is essentially an extension of the owner. He or she is personally responsible for all debts incurred on behalf of the business, i.e., liability does not stop with the exhaustion of the business assets. Besides owning all the assets used in the business and being liable for all the obligations incurred on its behalf, the owner may possess most of the knowledge and skill that determines the success of the business. The credit analyst must consider what would happen if the owner becomes incapacitated or dies.

It the owner dies there may be the added complication of waiting for estate settlement in order to collect the debt. Or, if the business continues to be operated by the estate, the surviving spouse or other heir, the entire credit analysis picture may have changed.

Partnerships

About 8 percent of U.S. businesses are partnerships. A *partnership* may be either general or limited. Under the general form, each partner is considered by law to have an equal voice in managing the business and each partner can make commitments on behalf of the partnership. Each partner is personally liable for debts incurred by the other partner or partners within the normal range of partnership business activity.

A limited partnership has one or more limited partners and one or more general partners. The general partner has full authority to act on behalf of the partnership and has unlimited liability for the obligations of the partnership. The limited partners have no voice in management but also have limited liability. Their liability is limited to the amount of their investment.

Although the problem usually is not as great as in a proprietorship, the credit analyst still must be concerned with the question of continuity of the business should a general partner become ill or die. When a general partner dies the partnership ceases to exist, though it may be a simple matter to form a successor partnership. In fact, it should be spelled out in the partnership agreement what is to be done regarding liquidation of assets or formation of a new partnership if one partner dies. However, many partnerships operate on an informal basis with no written partnership agreement. The credit analyst should determine what provisions, if any, the partnership has made in the event of the death of a partner.

A joint venture is a form of partnership that is formed for a single purpose. Usually a joint venture is dissolved when its purpose is accomplished. It may be either a general or limited partnership. Since it normally has limited existence, the credit analyst should take particular care that the partners are willing to individually guarantee any loans.

Corporations

Approximately 14 percent of the businesses in the U.S. are corporations. Almost all large firms are corporations, producing approximately 87 percent of the total business revenues in the U.S. A *corporation* is a legal entity separate and apart from its owners or founders. It gains its powers through a state charter. Exceptions to this are in the field of finance. Many savings associations, for example, have federal charters.

The corporate form of ownership has several advantages. First, it has unlimited life. The death of an owner (stockholder, or member in the case of mutually owned corporations) does not end the corporation. Second, ownership can be transferred easily and rapidly, particularly where the shares of stock in the corporation are traded in an active secondary market. This feature also facilitates raising new equity capital since the corporation can sell additional shares from time to time.

Third, the owners of a corporation have limited liability. Ordinarily they cannot lose more than they have invested in the corporation. Thus they cannot be held individually liable for the corporation's debts. However, it is common practice for lenders to small corporations to require the personal endorsements of major stockholders.

JUDGING MANAGEMENT EFFECTIVENESS

No matter what the organizational form of the business to which the loan is made, the judgments of the people operating the business may be the primary determinant as to whether or not the loan is repaid. A well-capitalized firm with marketable products or services can go bankrupt in the midst of good economic times due to poor managerial decisions.

Most of the focus of financial statement analysis is on judging management effectiveness. Personal discussions with the borrower also help form this judgment. If the business has not been in existence for a long period of time, or if the management is new to the business, or if it has recently entered new lines of activity, judging management effectiveness will be more complex and less precise. In such a situation, it may be desirable to require biographical data, including business history, of all key management people in the business. In addition, personal visits to the place of business may be helpful.

Visiting the Place of Business

An experienced credit officer may gain a significant amount of understanding about how well a firm is managed by visiting the place of business. An applicant for credit should be willing to accept a visit and provide a tour of the facilities.

The credit officer should note if employees seem to be performing effectively. Are the functions of the business well organized? Is the general appearance neat and orderly? Is there evidence of excessive expenditures such as delivery equipment capable of handling several times the firm's normal needs? Is inventory adequate? Excessive? Outdated or spoiled?

If the firm is in a retailing industry, a visit during a normally busy period may indicate the strength of its business as well as the effectiveness of the sales staff. In the case of a manufacturing firm, particular note should be taken of the equipment and production layout. Is it modern? Is it orderly? Does the equipment appear well maintained?

COLLATERAL

Collateral was probably the first addition to the original three C's of credit analysis. A lender requires collateral on many loans, including commercial loans, in order to provide protection from loss if the borrower fails to repay all or part of a loan. However, the strength of a loan should not be measured by the value of the collateral. The strength of a loan depends on the borrower's ability to generate cash sufficient to repay the loan (the borrower's capacity) and the borrower's determination to repay the loan (character). A lender never wants to have to liquidate collateral to recover a loan, but that is preferable to holding a defaulted, unsecured note.

The pledge of collateral puts pressure on many borrowers to repay or face losing essential assets. Here, pledging collateral may be considered a step that encourages discipline in the repayment of a loan. The credit analyst must understand the various forms of collateral, although this understanding will be limited to basic considerations where some forms of collateral are concerned. This is because at one time or another almost any type of asset may be offered as security for a business loan. The discussion here is limited to fixed assets other than real estate, inventory and accounts receivable.

Fixed Assets

An outside appraisal may be required to estimate the value of equipment or manufacturing facilities if these are of a specialized nature. Market quotations should be available on standard types of equipment such as trucks and tractors. However, the value the lender is interested in is liquidation value–how much could be derived from a forced sale? This value may be far below replacement cost, original cost or the book value on the firm's records.

Once the liquidating value of a fixed asset is estimated, the percentage of that value which can be loaned must be determined. Few lenders will advance more than 80 percent of liquidating value because of the potential for such values to decline in a period of economic recession. Another reason for this cushion of 20 percent or so is that if the borrower fails in business and ceases operation, a period of time will elapse before the asset can be claimed and sold by the lender. During this time interest continues to build on the loan, in effect increasing the amount the lender needs to recover to break even.

Inventory

When the credit officer visits the place of business, careful note should be taken of inventories. This should be done whether or not inventories are being pledged, in order to judge the effectiveness with which inventories are managed. Besides visual verification of quantities, physical condition and degree of obsolescence, if any, should be noted.

From the standpoint of credit analysis, inventory loans that are made under floor plan arrangements are the least complicated. The inventory items normally have broad marketability and values are easily established. The lender has a record of each item, including serial numbers and descriptions. Many other forms of inventory pose much greater problems for the credit analyst.

Raw materials used in a manufacturing or production process frequently experience wide fluctuations in price. Commodities such as grains, cocoa and sugar may rise sharply in price if a shortage seems apparent and fall dramatically when fear of the shortage fades. A processor who bought large amounts of a commodity at high prices may be in the position of trying to pledge the commodity when prices are low.

The liquidating value of finished goods also may be far below their cost to the manufacturer. A dressmaker who guessed wrong on this year's styles may have storerooms full of merchandise which can be sold only at 1/3 or 1/4 of cost. A publisher may have thousands of copies of a book that was expected to be a best seller but which can be sold only if priced at 25 cents per copy.

Work in process may be particularly complex to evaluate. How valuable is a half-finished lawn mower when the manufacturer ceases operations because of inability to meet financial obligations? Most lenders place little if any value on work in process in determining how much a business may borrow.

The methods used by the borrower to account for inventory should be understood by the credit analyst. Chapter 1 pointed out the differences between LIFO and FIFO accounting. Inventory acounting is a complex process, however, and should be studied at some length by the analyst.

Accounts Receivable

In estimating the collateral value of accounts receivable, the analyst must consider the financial strength of the borrower's customers. The borrower may have sold to weak customers on credit terms in order to bolster sales. Consequently, a large portion of the borrower's receivables may be past due.

The first step in evaluating receivables is to prepare an aging schedule. The schedule will show the percentage of credit customers at the time the schedule was prepared that have missed taking the discount (if available) and what percentage is past due. A sample aging schedule is shown in Figure 8-1.

Figure 8-1. Accounts Receivable Aging Schedule

Age of Account	Percent of Total Value
0-10 days	58%
11-30 days	27%
31-45 days	10%
46-60 days	3%
Over 60 days	2%

If it is assumed that the firm whose receivables appear in Figure 8-1 sells on terms of 2/10, net 30, then 58 percent of the trade debt owed the firm may be paid in time to receive the 2 percent discount.[2] An additional 27 percent may pay within 30 days. While 15 percent of the trade debt is late, it is probable that the 10 percent in the 31-45 day category offers no problem.

The ability to pay in time to take a discount is a very important indicator of the financial strength of the borrower's customers. Missing discounts is very costly. It should be assumed that if a customer does not pay by the tenth day, and thus misses the discount, payment will be made on the thirtieth day. After missing the discount, there is no reason to pay until the day before the account becomes overdue. Thus,

---

[2]This means that if the bill is paid within 10 days of the invoice date, 2 percent can be deducted from the bill. After 10 days and up to 30 days, the face or net amount of the bill is due.

the customer has retained use of the funds for 20 days. However, since the debt could have been liquidated for 98 percent of the total on the tenth day, the customer retained 98 percent for 20 days at a cost of 2 percent. The annualized cost of these funds, assuming a $100 invoice amount, is computed as follows:

$$\frac{\$2}{\$98} \times \frac{365 \text{ days}}{20} = 37.2\%$$

Missing the discount and incurring an effective cost in terms of an annualized rate of 37.2 percent may indicate financial weakness. At least it suggests inattentive management. Of course, the analyst also should determine whether the borrowing firm takes advantage of discounts.

Accounts past due may be eliminated by a lender in determining the total amount of receivables qualifying as collateral. Depending on the strength of the borrower's customers and other considerations, some amount less than face value will be advanced. Other aspects of accounts receivable lending should be noted by reviewing the sample policy at the end of Chapter 6.

SOURCES OF CREDIT INFORMATION

Credit information can include almost any information available about a company or its owners and managers. Time limitations will apply to gathering credit information, so the analyst should make sure that he or she pursues the most informative sources.

The financial statements of the company are essential sources of credit information. The analysis of financial statements (see Chapter 5) is the process of turning the information in the financial statements into its most usable form. Other sources which are discussed elsewhere in this textbook are personal interviews, visits to the place of business and the lender's own records. In addition, the lending institution should look to trade creditors, other lenders and credit reporting agencies for information about a business applying for credit.

TRADE REFERENCES

The businesses that sell to the applicant firm can be excellent sources of candid, precise answers as to how well the firm meets its obligations.

152   *Commercial Lending Basics*

Questions the analyst will ask the trade reference include:

- Does the firm pay for orders in time to gain discounts?
- Is the firm late in making payments and, if so, what percentage of payments are late?
- How large is the firm's average account?
- Do you have other background which would be helpful in a credit-granting decision?

When the credit analyst contacts the credit manager or other employee of the trade reference, the analyst should first establish his or her identity, the identity of the lending institution and the reason for requesting the information. If the contact is in writing, these points should be clearly set forth. No information should be requested which is beyond the scope of analysis pertinent to the loan application.

All information should be treated with absolute confidentiality, no matter what its source. If any information is misused, word will spread rapidly among credit managers in the area and the analyst will soon find difficulty gaining credit information. Usually, trade references are happy to provide credit information. From time to time they themselves seek information.

OTHER LENDERS

The applicant probably has done business–maintained accounts and borrowed–with other financial intermediaries. Loan balances may be outstanding at the time the analyst is seeking information. It is not uncommon for businesses to have two or more banking relationships.

Banks commonly exchange credit information and have done so for many years. Robert Morris Associates, the national association of bank commercial loan and credit officers, long ago established a code of ethics to govern the exchange of credit information among banks (see the Appendix). Lending institutions just entering the field of commercial lending (as well as consumer lending) will have increasing need to interact with banks regarding the exchange of credit information; observing the Robert Morris Associates' Code may be appropriate.

CREDIT REPORTING AGENCIES

Several organizations operate on a national basis providing credit reporting services. For example, the National Association of Credit Management provides information about the payment records of firms. The information consists of the experience of trade creditors who have extended credit to the firm in question.

Specialized agencies provide credit information about firms in specific industrial classifications. One example is the Lumbermen's Association. Another is the Lyon Furniture Mercantile Agency that will provide information about firms in the furniture, home appliance, department store, funeral and interior decoration industries.

Local offices of credit bureaus may provide credit information about firms doing business locally. Usually, however, credit bureaus limit their information to individuals. Nonetheless, they are valuable sources because it will be desirable in many cases to obtain credit reports on principal individuals in a company.

Of all the credit reporting agencies, the best known is Dun and Bradstreet. It collects and disseminates credit information on more than four million firms.

Dun and Bradstreet Information Report

Lending institutions commonly use the Dun and Bradstreet Business Information Report. A sample report for a hypothetical company is shown in Figure 8-2.

The subscriber number appears on the upper right corner of the report. That is the number assigned to Dun and Bradstreet's customer who purchased the report. The DUNS number on the upper left of the report is the number assigned to the firm which is the subject of the report. The SIC number in the upper center is the Standard Industrial Classification number. This is a classification system devised by the U.S. government.

Under the Summary heading in the upper right, the rating of BB1 is from the Dun and Bradstreet rating system. The two letters indicate the financial strength of the firm, i.e., net worth is from $200,000 to $299,999. The lowest rating is HH for a firm with less than $5,000 net worth and 5A is the highest for a firm with net worth over $50 million. The 1 following BB indicates the firm's credit rating is high (1 is high, 2 is good, 3 is fair and 4 is limited).

The balance of the Summary section shows at a glance several items of information which may be important. The hypothetical company in Figure 8-2 has a long and positive history, appears to be in good financial condition and its business has been in a positive trend.

The "Special Events" section is not included in every report. In the case of the hypothetical company in Figure 8-2, two special events were noted: a burglary and an expansion of merchandise lines.

The "Payments Reported" section shows how the company has met its recent trade credit obligations. The hypothetical company's payment record shows no late payments, although it missed one discount (ppt stands for prompt). "High Credit" is the largest amount owed at one time.

Figure 8-2

© *Dun & Bradstreet, Inc.*

This report has been prepared for:

BE SURE NAME, BUSINESS AND ADDRESS MATCH YOUR FILE.

ANSWERING INQUIRY

SUBSCRIBER: 008-001042

CONSOLIDATED REPORT

```
DUNS: 00-647-3261              DATE PRINTED            SUMMARY
BEAUMONT & HUNT INC           OCT 15 198-            RATING     BB1
                              DEPARTMENT STORE
120 LEMOINE AVE                                     STARTED    1956
AUGUSTA, GA   30901           SIC NO.               PAYMENTS   SEE BELOW
     TEL: 404 872-9664        53 11                 SALES      $1,600,000
                                                    WORTH   F  $261,791
                                                    EMPLOYS    20
DANIEL T BEAUMONT, PRES                             HISTORY    CLEAR
                                                    CONDITION  STRONG
                                                    TREND      UP
```

SPECIAL EVENTS

09/10/8- Kevin Hunt, Sec-Treas, reported a $3,000 merchandise loss in Sep 8 burglary. Loss is fully insured.

05/17/8- CHANGES: Subject recently expanded its line of merchandise with the addition of sporting goods.

PAYMENTS   (Amounts may be rounded to nearest figure in prescribed ranges)

REPORTED	PAYING RECORD	HIGH CREDIT	NOW OWES	PAST DUE	SELLING TERMS	LAST SALE WITHIN
09/8-	Disc	15000	5000	-0-	2 10 N30	1 Mo
08/8-	Ppt	7500	500	-0-	30	2-3 Mos
	Ppt	5000	2500	-0-	30	1 Mo
07/8-	Disc	10000	2500	-0-	30	2-3 Mos
	Ppt	2500	1000	-0-	30	2-3 Mos
	Ppt	1000	-0-	-0-	EOM	2-3 Mos
02/8-	Disc	10000	500	-0-	2 10 N30	1 Mo
	Ppt	2500	500	-0-	2 10 N30	1 Mo
	Ppt	1000	-0-	-0-	30	2-3 Mos

FINANCE

02/15/8-   Fiscal statement dated Oct 31 198—.

```
Cash              $      75,000   Accts Pay         $    140,510
Accts Rec              110,746    Accruals                48,636
Inventory              285,465    Fed & Other Taxes       26,714
Prepaid                  1,240    ---------------
          ---------------
Current                472,451    Current                215,860
Fixt & Equip             5,200    CAPITAL STOCK           50,000
                                  RETAINED EARNINGS      211,791
          ---------------                        ---------------
Total Assets           477,651    Total                  477,651
```

Annual sales $1,600,000; net income $48,000; monthly rent $2,500. Lease expires 198-. Fire insurance on mdse & fixt $300,000.

Accountant: Fred Mitchell, Augusta, GA. Prepared from books without audit.

--0--

UPDATE: On Aug 10 198-, Daniel T Beaumont, Pres, said nine months sales through July 31 were up 10%, profits rising. Concern now employs 20.

On Feb 14, 198- Kevin J Hunt reported sales and profits in fiscal quarter ended Jan 31 as above those of prior year period because of an upsurge in local economy. He expects full year sales to exceed $1.7 million.

PUBLIC FILINGS

03/25/8-   On Mar 17 198 , a suit in the amount of $250 was entered against subject by A Henry Associates, Augusta, GA (Docket #27511). Cause of action goods sold and delivered.

05/28/8-   On May 21 198-, a financing statement (#741170) was filed listing subject as debtor and NCR Corp, Dayton, OH as secured party. Collateral consists of equipment.

08/10/8-   Kevin J Hunt reported action filed by A Henry Associates was due to defective merchandise and had been settled. Court records reveal the suit was withdrawn.

BANKING

02/15/8-   Balances average moderate five figures. Non-borrowing account. Relations satisfactory. Account opened Jun 1956.

(CONTINUED)

Figure 8-2

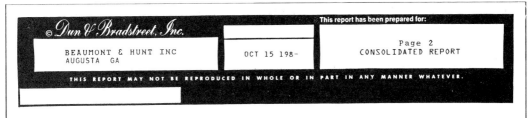

© *Dun & Bradstreet, Inc.*

BEAUMONT & HUNT INC
AUGUSTA GA

OCT 15 198-

This report has been prepared for:

Page 2
CONSOLIDATED REPORT

HISTORY
02/15/8-
DANIEL T BEAUMONT, PRES   KEVIN J HUNT, SEC-TREAS
DIRECTOR(S): THE OFFICER(S)
Incorporated Georgia. May 21 1956. Authorized capital consists of 200 shares
common stock, no par value.
DANIEL T BEAUMONT born 1926 married. Graduate University of Pennsylvania.
1947-56 general manager Raymor Department Store, Atlanta, GA. 1956 formed subject
with K Hunt.
KEVIN J HUNT born 1925 married. Graduate Northwestern University. 1946-50
general manager United Dry Goods Inc. 1950-56 merchandising manager, Raymor
Department Store, Atlanta, GA.

OPERATION
Department store retailing dry goods, notions, household items, hardware,
confections, toys, and sundry items. Prices in low to moderate range. Sales made to
local trade on cash (40%) and revolving credit (60%) basis.
EMPLOYEES: 20, including the officers.
FACILITIES: Rents 6,000 sq. ft. on ground floor and basement of multi story
brick building in downtown area. Premises neat.

The "Now Owes" column allows comparison of latest balances with "High Credit" amounts. If the "Now Owes" balance is the same or near the "High Credit" figure the company may be close to exhausting its credit. The company in the sample report owes far less than its high credit amounts.

The hypothetical company is current with all its accounts. If a past due amount appeared in this column that was small compared to the high credit amount, it might be due to a lost billing, a dispute over an invoice or a similar reason.

The "Finance" section consists of the company's balance sheet, as of the date given, and other pertinent financial information. Any updated sales reports are important to note.

The "Public Filings" section is included in a report only if a development has occurred which justifies reporting. The "Banking," "History" and "Operations" sections conclude the report.

In addition to its Business Information Report, Dun and Bradstreet provides several other services that may be helpful to the credit analyst. One of these, the "Key Account Report Service," provides a comprehensive report exclusively for the subscriber making the inquiry.

OTHER CREDIT INFORMATION SOURCES

In some situations the analyst may gain information from competitors and customers of the applicant. Confidentiality is always vital in using such information.

Public information is available in many forms. These include court records of suits or other actions, records of property transfers, Uniform Commercial Code filings and trade directories. Information sources at the federal level include the Securities and Exchange Commission, the Interstate Commerce Commission, and the Federal Communications Commission (for broadcasting businesses).

Investment manuals, particularly those published by Moodys Investment Services, Inc., and the Standard and Poor's Corporation, can provide useful information about large corporations. The investment reports published by the various investment firms such as E.F. Hutton and Dean Witter Reynolds, Inc., can also provide useful statistics and insights regarding large, publicly held corporations.

JUDGMENT FACTOR IN CREDIT ANALYSIS

Who conducts the credit analysis in the commercial lending process? It may be the loan officer who will make the recommendation to either make or not to make a loan. It may be someone who assists the loan officer and spends most of his or her time doing credit analysis. Whoever the person, he or she needs a high level of technical understanding. The need for some depth in accounting, economics and financial analysis has been stressed in previous sections. Also, however, the analyst must develop an educated "judgment."

Many aspects of credit analysis do not lend themselves to precise numerical evaluation. Character, for example, cannot be assigned a number. The credit analyst learns to look for indicators, signs of possible problems that may emerge in the future. Some examples of such signs include:

- Unexplained switching of trade suppliers;
- A change in the timing of a seasonal loan request;
- Loss of a major customer;
- Lack of effort to create management succession;
- Sudden entry into new endeavors;
- Changes in the personal habits of key personnel;
- Loss of a key product line.

This list is intended to suggest the importance of experienced judgment. It could be expanded at great length by an experienced analyst. Application of such judgment can avoid many lending arrangements which later prove disappointing.

SUMMARY

Credit analysis is the process of determining, with as much certainty as time and available information allow, whether a borrower will be able and willing to repay a loan. Credit analysis is normally viewed as having several elements. These subdivisions may be as few as the original three C's of character, capacity and capital, or as many as the analyst feels appropriate.

Other subdivisions and considerations include conditions (primarily economic), industry characteristics, forms of business organization (proprietorship, partnership or corporation), management effectiveness and collateral. In business lending, collateral usually consists of fixed assets used in the business, inventory or accounts receivable.

Adequate sources of information are critical to a successful credit analysis. Important sources include trade references, other lenders and credit reporting services. Dun and Bradstreet reports are particularly significant in this latter category.

There are many other credit services that experience will teach the analyst to use. The analyst develops a great deal of such technical skill over time, but perhaps as important is the development of experienced judgment. Applying experienced judgment may help prevent many disappointing lending situations.

CHAPTER QUESTIONS

1. Why is the assessment of character so important in credit analysis?
2. What are the distinguishing characteristics of proprietorships, partnerships and corporations?
3. In credit analysis, "conditions" is a broad term. What does it include?
4. What is an accounts receivable aging schedule?
5. What are three of the items of information shown on a Dun & Bradstreet Business Information Report?
6. What is the "judgment factor" in credit analysis?

9

The Lending
Decision Process

OBJECTIVES

After reading Chapter 9, you should be able to:

- Describe the sequence of the lending decision process;
- List five important items of information that the interviewer should obtain in the initial interview;
- Explain when and how a turndown should be made;
- Cite the steps to be taken immediately after the initial interview;
- Describe the purpose of the credit report;
- Name the three major elements of loan structure;
- Explain the role of the loan committee in the lending decision process.

Lending institutions new to the field of commercial lending cannot expect to develop a high quality portfolio of commercial loans without a significant effort. As previous chapters have indicated, the people responsible for the commercial lending function should possess both knowledge and experience. Also, the organization must devote the time and expense required to establish policy, to install essential systems and to enhance the business development effort.

Even though an institution may have high capability and thorough preparation, the process of developing good lending opportunities may be slow. The competition for large and financially strong borrowers is intense. Winning over a meaningful number of high quality borrowers may be an expensive and extended process.

At the other extreme, it is likely there will be a large number of applicants from the low quality end of the borrowing spectrum. Most of these applicants will have little chance for success in business, even if they are granted extensive, liberally structured loans. The weakness of these applicants, due to their financial inadequacies or lack of business understanding, normally will be so evident that they can be turned down without a large expenditure of time and talent.

Between the high quality and the low quality sectors there is a large group of business firms from which most of the institution's commercial lending opportunities will come. The nature of these firms was described in Chapter 7. They are small and are run by realistic people who work very hard to make their firms successful. Many of them depend to some degree on borrowed funds and have an insufficient number of borrowing alternatives.

The decision to lend or not to lend to the applicants from this large group seldom will be clear cut. The need to develop a high quality portfolio of loans from the applications drawn from this group places tremendous importance on properly conducting the lending decision process.

INITIAL INTERVIEW

The commercial lending decision process begins with a personal interview, normally at the lender's office. This may or may not be the applicant's first contact with the lender. A representative of the lender may have called previously at the applicant's place of business or some prior lending or deposit relationship may exist. Thus, the amount of information known to the loan officer or other interviewer before the interview begins will be different in each case. Nonetheless, the initial interview is the first meeting to discuss a specific credit request.

There will be occasions when a potential borrower will visit the lender's office without previously making an appointment. While this may suggest an unsophisticated approach to borrowing, it does not necessarily mean the potential borrower may not qualify for a loan. However, an unannounced visit may take place when the potential borrower has just been turned down elsewhere or was offered credit under terms considered undesirable. Or, the potential borrower may be conducting a "fishing expedition" among local lenders to get an idea what credit will be available if a venture is undertaken. In most cases, it will be better to ask the business person to set an appointment for the initial interview rather than attempt the interview with no preparation on either side.

CONDUCTING THE INTERVIEW

The interviewer should attempt to gain as much information as possible during the initial interview. This should be done in a friendly and positive manner. Respect should be shown for the applicant's business situation and ideas. Complex terminology not familiar to the applicant should be avoided.

There is the danger that the interviewer, who is very sensitive to the risk of making an undesirable loan, may appear overly negative. The interviewer may seem to be looking for that one answer that will justify rejecting the application. Needless to say, if the business person leaves with this feeling, more harm than good has come from the interview.

Saying No

If a loan should not be made, it is better to make this determination in the initial interview than after both the lender and the applicant have invested extensive time and effort. Thus, as many pertinent questions as possible should be asked during the initial interview. When the interviewer recognizes that the loan should not be made, the applicant should be informed.

The turndown should be made clearly and as politely as possible. This should be true no matter when in the lending decision process the turndown takes place. Many weak applicants are aware of the shortcomings of their proposals. Others, however, will feel their applications are justifiable and their disappointment can lead to harsh feelings if the turndown is not explained in terms they can accept.

The turndown, if it is made in terms acceptable to the applicant, may not terminate the interview. At all times, the interviewer should consider the possibility of developing new business. Even though this specific loan cannot be made, other credit needs of the borrower may justify consideration. Or, the interviewer may suggest other alternatives to the rejected loan. For example, a deposit relationship may be developed with the applicant. At any rate, the applicant should not leave uninformed about ways in which the institution may be helpful.

WHAT TO LEARN DURING THE INTERVIEW

The interviewer should learn as much as possible in the initial interview, but it is unlikely that all data necessary for the loan decision can be gathered at this one meeting. The exception to this rule on gathering data, of course, is the loan application which obviously must be turned down.

The interviewer should use a checklist to try to assure that as many questions as possible are answered during the initial meeting. In addition, notes should be taken to assure that important points are not forgotten. The checklist should begin with information about the borrower–type of business, business name, location, organization form, and names and addresses of the principals. Once this basic information is acquired, the questions should produce more discussion by the applicant than by the interviewer.

Loan Purpose

The first substantive question during the interview should ask how the loan proceeds will be used. If the loan purpose conflicts with commercial loan policy, such as a loan for some speculative purpose not acceptable to the lender, the turndown should follow immediately. A clear explanation should be given as to why the lender chooses not to make loans of that type. Examples might be a loan for inventory speculation or a loan to form a new business where the applicant's capital is very "thin." In this latter case, the interviewer should make sure the applicant is aware of the Small Business Administration guaranteed loan program. The lending institution might be able to make the loan under that program.

The stated loan purpose may be acceptable but it may be given in vague terms, such as "We want to add some inventory." The interviewer must encourage a more precise answer. For example, if the applicant represents a retailer, does the retailer intend to expand existing lines or add new ones? Is this a seasonal expansion (calling for a line of credit) or a permanent expansion (which may require intermediate-term credit such as a revolving credit agreement)? Who supplies the merchandise? Are there alternative sources of the merchandise?

If the stated loan purpose is vague, the interviewer should consider asking the applicant to write down precisely the intended use of the funds and all attendant considerations. This should be in the form of a loan proposal to be returned to the interviewer along with other information that may be requested.

There will be applicants who state one purpose for a loan that actually will be used for a different purpose. This may be unintentional. The applicant simply may not understand the nature of cash flow within the firm. It may be that the firm's liquidity was dissipated last year to pay for an addition to the building. Now the firm may be having difficulty paying its trade creditors. The firm may be applying for a short-term inventory loan. The interviewer should recognize that if the lender makes the short-term loan, it will be injecting itself into the position now held by the trade creditors. When the short-term loan comes due, it is unlikely that the firm will be able to repay the lender.

The firm actually needs a longer-term loan to offset the long-term use (the building addition). A mortgage or term loan might be possible.

A few applicants may purposely misstate the intended use of loan proceeds knowing that their desired use will be unacceptable. While this intent may not become apparent to the interviewer, subsequent credit analysis may suggest financial weakness, business problems or character flaws that will discourage the lender from making the loan.

Loan Amount

The amount of the loan may be stated when the purpose is given. If the applicant has a well thought out proposal, he or she probably knows the amount that will be required. On some occasions an applicant may indicate a desire to borrow as much as possible. This puts the burden on the lender to specify an amount based on the borrowing power of the applicant. The amount may be more or less than actually needed. This approach might be appropriate if the purpose was to establish a line of credit, but in most cases it would be preferable for the applicant to determine the amount of the request.

Repayment Source

Every business loan should have a primary and a secondary, or backup, repayment source. Failure by a lender to require and secure a secondary source for each loan will sooner or later result in problem loans for the lender.

The primary source may be considered the intended source, the one which both lender and borrower expect to produce repayment. It should be tied as closely as possible to the use of the loan proceeds. For example, repayment of a seasonal inventory loan is expected to come from the cash generated by the sale of the inventory, and repayment of an equipment loan is expected to be made from the cash flow generated as a result of the firm's possession and operation of the equipment.

The secondary source of repayment in the case of the equipment loan probably would be through repossession and sale of the equipment since the lender normally would have retained title pending full payment from the borrower. The secondary source in the case of the seasonal loan may be any form of collateral, including the inventory. It may be a cosigner or guarantor.

What is the secondary repayment source in the case of an unsecured loan? It could be said that there is no secondary source since no collateral is taken. However, if a firm is so strong financially that it can borrow on an unsecured basis, then it has an abundance of liquid assets that could be converted to cash to fulfill the loan if the primary source of repayment fails.

During the initial interview, the lender's representative should begin the process of determining whether or not a viable secondary repayment source exists. In basic terms, all business loan repayments can come from only three general sources: 1) sale of assets, 2) increases in other debts and 3) increases in owner's equity through additions or from retention of earnings (see Chapter 2 for a review of the balance sheet discussion).

These simple considerations of the interview framework can help the interviewer and the applicant in thinking about the loan; the interviewer in his or her initial assessment of the strength or weakness of the potential loan; and the applicant in his or her understanding of the requirements that the lender will impose. If, for example, the loan is to finance a form of inventory that may sharply decline in value, both the interviewer and the applicant should recognize that the inventory itself will not adequately secure the loan. Does the firm have other assets that it can pledge and that the lender can control in order to provide the additional collateral? The interviewer should ask if these assets are free of other encumbrances.

If it appears that no other assets will be available to provide the secondary source of payment, the possibility of obtaining other borrowing sources to provide the funds to repay this loan should be considered. Ordinarily it is a weak approach to debt repayment to look to another source of credit. However, this is essentially what is done when a guarantor or cosigner backs the loan. If they are looked to for payment, they, in effect, lend the firm the funds to repay the debt.

The third general source of debt repayment is through additions to owner's equity, either from retained earnings or additions by the owners. In the short term, retained earnings will seldom be enough to provide a meaningful secondary repayment source. In the long term, retained earnings–as part of cash flow (see Chapter 2)–are looked to as the primary source of repayment for intermediate- and long-term loans, so the secondary source must be other than retained earnings.

Future additions of equity by owners can serve as the secondary source of repayment. Lenders frequently require the personal guarantees of owners on business loans, including those of large stockholders of closely held corporations.

Repayment Schedule

The applicant should set forth the timing for repayment of the loan. Just as it is most desirable that the primary source of repayment be tied to the utilization or disposition of the asset financed, the timing of repayment should, if possible, coincide with the generation of funds from the asset financed. A seasonal inventory loan should be set for repayment when the inventory turns into cash through sale and collection of accounts receivable, not three or six months later. If the payment date is past the time when the inventory turns into cash, there is danger that the funds will go to another use and the lender will be holding a problem loan when the scheduled repayment date arrives.

The applicant's repayment plan should be realistic. If, for example, it is based on the assumption that a large increase in sales is forthcoming, the interviewer should be skeptical if this expectation does not fit past sales patterns.

History of the Business

The interviewer should ask how long the business has been in operation, how long the present management has been in charge, and for such biographical information as age, background and experience of the principals. Other pertinent historical information would include the length of time present products (or services) have been offered, how the firm has met competition, whether or not it has experienced labor problems, and whether or not it has maintained long relationships with major customers. A good historical summary can add meaning to the financial analysis process.

Banking Relationships

The initial interview should identify the financial institutions where the applicant has accounts and loans, if any. Historically, many firms have their accounts and loans with commercial banks. In recent years, firms have done their "banking" at institutions other than commercial banks. Many smaller firms keep their liquid funds in money market funds or certificates at thrift institutions. And, as Chapter 1 discussed, there are numerous alternative sources from which businesses can borrow.

The interviewer should ask why the applicant wants to change from its present financial institution if it presently has a borrowing relationship. This should not be passed over lightly because considerations may emerge that will impact on the new lender's decision of whether or not to lend to the applicant. If the applicant was refused a loan by the institution that had previously granted credit, the interviewer should find out why. The interviewer should inquire as to any presently outstanding loans, unpaid balances, due dates and collateral, if any.

The interviewer should point out that the institution expects a deposit relationship if the loan is made. Of course, if a compensating balance requirement is imposed, the deposit relationship is automatic.

Plant and Equipment

The applicant should be asked about the nature and capability of the firm's physical facilities. The applicant should be informed that a visit to the place of business by a representative of the lender may be required.

Insurance

The applicant may not know the exact insurance coverages and their extent. The best way to check on this important item may be to ask the applicant to have the firm's insurance agent call the interviewer. This will not only produce exact amounts of coverage, but will also verify that the coverages are in force.

The interviewer will want to know that insurance coverage applies to all major risks and that the amounts are adequate. Besides property and personal liability coverages, it may be important for the firm to carry life insurance on those individuals who are largely responsible for the continued operation of the firm. If the loan is made, the lender may require key-person insurance and also require that the lender be named beneficiary under the key-person policies.

CLOSING THE INTERVIEW

The interviewer should not expect to obtain all pertinent information in the initial interview. The applicant may not have answers to some questions without checking records or consulting other members of the company. Also, the demands of time may limit what can be done in the initial interview. However, if the time was used effectively and if the application deserves further consideration, the applicant should leave the interview with a written list of information and documents to provide the interviewer. These will include the firm's financial statements, probably for the most recent three years. Personal financial statements of the principals also may be required. In addition, the lending institution may require a written loan proposal or completed loan application, a borrowing resolution if the firm is a corporation,[1] evidence of insurance and an aging schedule of accounts receivable. The exact requirements will vary from loan to loan, but the interviewer should make sure that there is no confusion about what is required before the applicant leaves the initial interview.

AFTER THE INTERVIEW

Immediately following the interview, the notes taken by the interviewer should be organized and expanded as necessary in order to portray all of the factual information developed during the interview. This also helps locate any unanswered questions that must be clarified. Since other people in the organization may work with the loan application when the interviewer is not present to explain the notes, care should be taken to assure that the notes are understandable and meaningful.

The next immediate step should be creation of the credit file. The *credit file* will be the central information source for everyone who works with the application. The file should be maintained even if the loan presently being applied for is rejected. Future business with the applicant may be possible, so all of the information gathered as a result of the initial application may be useful.

In addition to a copy of the interviewer's notes, the credit file will contain copies of all correspondence and memoranda regarding the application, copies of all financial statements and the results of analyzing the statements, the history of the relationship with the applicant (if any), and a record of any other loans made to the applicant firm or any of its principals.

Although each lender will have its own system of filing and document storage, it is unlikely that documents such as signed notes, titles and warehouse receipts will be kept in the credit file. These should be maintained in a vault or other storage facility with limited access.

COLLECTING CREDIT INFORMATION

The collection of credit information begins in the initial interview. It continues as the applicant provides the financial statements and other

---

[1] The bylaws of a corporation will name by title those persons who are authorized to borrow on behalf of the corporation. The borrowing resolution sets this forth along with the name or names of those persons. It contains the seal of the corporation and is signed by the corporate secretary.

information which the interviewer requested. In addition, the collection of credit information will include as many of the procedures described in Chapter 8 as required by the particular application.

The type of loan applied for and the circumstances of the applicant will determine how extensive the collection of credit information will be. A seasonal loan should require less credit information than a revolving credit agreement. If an applicant is well known, has a lengthy and successful business history and is financially strong, less information is needed than if the application represents a new endeavor by a firm with limited financial resources.

CONDUCTING THE CREDIT ANALYSIS

The lending decision process, of which credit analysis is a large and important part, is a procedure of answering questions. At any point in the process an answer may determine that a loan will not be made. However, the further the process goes the more likely it is that the loan will be made, because the questions that should readily disqualify the application will be asked early in the initial interview. The credit analyst should not expect the evaluation of the credit information to produce obvious yes or no answers regarding desirability of making a given loan.

ANALYZING THE INFORMATION

Analysis of credit information attempts to answer the question "How risky would it be to lend to this applicant?" Most commercial loans are risky to some degree. Up to a certain risk level, a lender may justify granting a particular loan and attempt to compensate for the relatively high risk by charging a high rate of interest. Above that certain risk level, loans will not be granted. Thus, it can be said that credit analysis: 1) determines which loans will be made and which will not and 2) provides a ranking from low risk to high risk for those loans that are made, thus helping determine the rates of interest that will be charged.

The need to assess risk and thus decide if a loan should or should not be made and, if made, what interest rate is appropriate, underlies all credit analysis. This includes the effort to project economic conditions, the financial statement analysis described in Chapter 5, attempts to assess the character of potential borrowers and all of the other analytical considerations discussed thus far. Yet with all this analysis, the judgment of credit risk is quite arbitrary. The ratios computed for a given company might lead one credit analyst to consider a potential loan to the company as "very risky" while another analyst, viewing the same ratios, would consider the loan only "somewhat risky."

Risk-Rating Systems

In an effort to make credit analysis more scientific and to measure the elements of credit information, some commercial lending officers have devised risk-rating systems for commercial loans.[2] A risk-rating system places numerical values or weights on each item of information considered important in judging the risk of a potential loan.

Many of the systems are somewhat intricate, but a very simple system might work as follows: each important factor–liquidity, financial leverage, management ability, collateral, etc.–is assigned a value from 1 to 5, with 1 being best and 5 being worst. For example, if a firm's liquidity position is excellent, it would be rated 1.

Once ratings have been assigned to each factor they are totaled and divided by the number of factors. The resultant number is the overall rating for the loan. If it is above a predetermined level, say 3.5, the loan will not be considered. For the applicants that do qualify, the higher the numerical rating the higher the interest rate assigned to the loan.

Risk-rating systems do not totally eliminate the judgment factor. Someone must decide how the ratings will be assigned. Such systems, even with the judgment factor considered, do make the credit analysis process more uniform throughout a large organization and usually they allow credit analysis to be performed by less experienced personnel.

Computer Assisted Credit Analysis

A number of lending institutions, particularly large ones, have computerized much of the credit analysis process. It was pointed out in Chapter 5 that a large number of financial relationships could be calculated using a company's financial statements. The computer can make these calculations rapidly and more extensively than might the analyst.

Computer programs provide calculations of ratios, prepare pro forma statements and cash budgets, perform trend analysis and many other analytical steps. The analyst can vary the assumptions as to future economic conditions, sales levels or costs and rerun the program in order to test the sensitivity of the applicant's repayment ability under

---

[2] Stephen F. Sherrod, "An Objective Risk Rating System for Commercial Loans," *The Journal of Commercial Bank Lending*, November 1981, pp. 12-32.

each of these assumptions. It is probable that computer assisted credit analysis will become more important in the future.

PREPARING THE CREDIT REPORT

The results of the credit analysis should be set forth in a written credit report. In those financial institutions where the commercial lending activity is sufficiently large to justify specialization of functions, the credit analysis probably will not be performed by the loan officer. In these institutions, the credit analyst will be responsible for conveying the results of the credit analysis in precise, meaningful form to give the loan officer as much aid as possible in reaching a decision of whether or not a loan should be made. If the loan officer conducts the credit analysis, preparing the credit report will be valuable to him or her in bringing together all the results of the credit analysis. The report will also be an important item in the credit file.

The credit report should follow a structured format so that the items of information are in the same order from one report to the next. How much detail the report contains will depend on the format and style preferred by the institution and on the complexity of a given loan request. However, all pertinent information should be included. This will include the answers to the important questions asked during the initial interview, the results of checking the various sources of credit information and the consequences of the financial statement analysis. The approach followed by the institution may or may not require a recommendation at the end of the report. If credit reports are prepared by trainees or other junior personnel, the requirement to conclude with a recommendation can be an excellent training device.

LOAN STRUCTURE

The elements of a loan's structure include the interest rate, repayment terms and collateral, if any. When the loan officer becomes reasonably certain that the loan can be made, the elements of structure become important considerations. If a written loan proposal is to be submitted to a loan committee, the structure considered most appropriate by the presenting officer will be included in the proposal.

PRICING THE LOAN

Loan policy should define the method of determining the interest rate on commercial loans while leaving the loan officer some room to negotiate with the borrower. The officer must balance the desire to make the loan against the need to produce a reasonable profit. At times, the profit consideration may cause the loss of what otherwise could be a desirable loan. A competing lender may make the loan at a lower rate than the institution can justify. This will be a disappointment but it is preferable to making nonprofitable loans.

If the borrower does not have an alternate source of credit, but simply believes that his or her firm deserves a lower rate, then the negotiating and salesmanship skills of the loan officer will be called upon. In this activity there is no substitute for experience.

Floating Rates

The application of floating rates to commercial loans is becoming widespread. Several points of negotiation can emerge if a floating rate is to be applied. Assuming the base rate to be applied is the prime rate (see Chapter 6), the borrower may disagree with the spread above prime which the loan officer wants to assign. The borrower may also want a "cap," that is, a ceiling rate that will not be exceeded no matter how high interest rates may go. Or the borrower may object to a "floor" rate, which is the minimum rate which will be charged no matter how low rates may fall.

REPAYMENT TERMS

The commercial loan policy should set forth general maturity guidelines. Within these the loan officer should have some flexibility to tailor terms to fit specific situations. And, as stated earlier, the source and timing of repayment should be tied as closely as possible to the loan purpose. However, the lender does not want to "fall behind," that is, to find itself in a position where the remaining balance of a loan is greater than the value of the asset financed.

For example, the projected useful life of a piece of heavy equipment might be six years. At first thought a five-year repayment period might seem appropriate. However, if a major overhaul will be required at the end of three years to make the six-year life a reality, it could be that the loan balance at the end of three years is greater than the value of the equipment. It could also be that the borrower needs another loan to pay for the needed overhaul. The loan terms should be set initially so that the loan is retired largely, if not completely, before the overhaul is due.

STEPS REGARDING COLLATERAL

Before the final decision is made to grant the loan, the loan officer must make sure that collateral to be taken will adequately serve to secure the loan. If inventory is the collateral, inspection and perhaps an appraisal may be required. Also, a warehousing arrangement may be necessary. If accounts receivable are to serve as collateral, in addition to an aging schedule, the loan officer will want to verify at least the larger invoices against the borrower's accounts receivable ledger. Also the lender may want customer verification, by phone or letter, of perhaps 10 to 20 percent of the account balances.

If equipment is to be used as collateral it must be appraised by someone, preferably a professional, who is knowledgeable regarding the equipment. Also the loan officer must make sure the equipment can be monitored to prevent its disappearance and assure it is well maintained.

The above are only a few of the steps that may be required to make sure that collateral will adequately secure a loan. Many forms of property can serve as collateral and a number of procedures may be required for each.

PRESENTING THE PROPOSAL

An experienced loan officer probably will have authority to make loans up to a certain dollar amount if all policy requirements are met. Loans above a specified dollar amount or which require departure from policy will require the approval of one or more higher level officers or of a loan committee. This procedure will require the loan officer to prepare a loan proposal.

PRESENTATION

The proposal should be prepared in written form and follow an established format. It should include, in summary form, all of the pertinent aspects of the application. If more detail is needed on any points when the presentation is made, the loan officer will have the credit file and other information for reference.

The loan officer's recommendation is a vital part of the proposal. Normally the recommendation will be to make the loan. However, there may be occasions when a loan application is marginal and the loan officer wants the rejection to be at a higher level of authority.

LOAN COMMITTEE

Policy may require that loans above a certain dollar amount be presented to a loan committee. A large organization may have two levels of committees, with the senior committee passing judgment on only very large applications. However, senior committees probably will review loans made by the junior committee. If there are two committees, the membership of the senior committee probably will include members of the board of directors. If there is only one committee, it may or may not include one or more directors.

The purpose of the loan committee is to provide consistency in the lending decisions and quality in the loan portfolio. Group judgment should eliminate the biases that an individual might inject into the lending decisions and should also result in fewer mistakes than one person would make.

A smoothly functioning committee can be valuable in the lending decision process with the members contributing experience and knowledge of local situations that the loan officer may not possess. However, some aspects of the committee process may not be beneficial. A committee may become a bottleneck. Its members may want to discuss each item of each proposal at great length and, consequently, may not finish review of all proposals. The loan officer must then contact some applicants and point out that the decision regarding the loan must await the next committee meeting. This could result in a lost loan opportunity.

A "bottleneck" committee may have the effect of stifling the productivity of an experienced lending officer. On the other hand, a smoothly functioning committee that fulfills its responsibilities can enhance the lending officer's effectiveness.

SUMMARY

The lending decision process can best be viewed as a search for answers. This search begins in the initial interview. The interviewer should ask the applicant a number of important questions, the answer to any one of which could result in the rejection of the application. If a turndown must be made, it should be in terms clearly understandable to the applicant.

The answers which should be obtained in the initial interview include the purpose of the loan, the amount desired, the source of repayment, the repayment schedule, the history of the business and its principals, banking relationships, and information about plant, equipment and insurance.

If the application appears justifiable, collection and analysis of credit information will follow the initial interview. The results of the analysis should be set forth in a written credit report.

The next step in the lending decision process is to answer the question as to how best to structure the loan. The elements of structure include the interest rate, repayment terms and collateral required.

The loan amount may be within the approval limits of the loan officer in charge of the application. If not, he or she will make a presentation, in the form of a loan proposal, to higher ranking officers or a loan committee.

CHAPTER QUESTIONS

1. What are three important facts which should be learned in the initial loan interview?

2. If at some point in the lending decision process it is determined that the borrower cannot qualify, how soon after this determination should the turndown be made?

3. What are the three broad sources from which all business loans are repaid?

4. What is the purpose of a risk-rating system?

5. What are the elements of a loan's structure?

6. How should the loan committee enhance the lending decision process and how may it hinder the process?

10

Commercial Loan Administration

OBJECTIVES

After reading Chapter 10, you should be able to:

- List and explain four commercial lending documents;
- Outline procedures for follow-up with the borrower;
- Explain the value of the loan agreement to the lender;
- Cite the two major purposes of loan review;
- List five corrective actions that might be taken when a borrower shows evidence of financial difficulties;
- Briefly describe proceedings under Chapter 7 and Chapter 11 of the bankruptcy act.

The purpose of this chapter is to describe the important aspects of loan administration pertaining to commercial lending. So far, this textbook has been concerned largely with the knowledge that should be possessed, the analysis and investigation that should be conducted and other considerations involved in reaching the decision to lend or not to lend funds to a business. This chapter focuses on elements of the commercial lending function that result from the decision to grant a loan.

The importance of the administration of commercial loans should not be minimized. Commercial loans cannot be "put on the books" and then ignored. In fact, some commercial lending people believe that the most difficult part of the commercial lending function follows the decision to make the loan. However, the treatment given in this chapter to the administrative aspect of commercial lending is succinct and general. There are two reasons for this. First, this textbook is intended to be an introduction designed primarily to help develop concepts and a general understanding of commercial lending. It is not intended to explain the detailed work involved in day-to-day commercial lending activity.

Second, many of the elements of commercial loan administration, such as the forms required and their titles, regulations and practices, differ from state to state. In addition, the methods of conducting commercial lending differ from one organization to another. Also, codes and regulations change from time to time and new approaches to making certain types of loans will emerge.

DOCUMENTATION

Proper documentation is vital to a successful commercial lending operation. The proceeds of a loan should not be made available to a borrower until all necessary documentation is in place.

Much of the documentation required in commercial lending is determined by the Uniform Commercial Code (UCC). While its major provisions are more or less constant from state to state, each state has adopted its own version of the UCC. Also, some states have not adopted some changes from the original 1962 version which the sponsors of the Code proposed in 1972. Individuals involved in commercial lending should become familiar with provisions of the Code applicable for their state.

Some of the documentary items required in certain situations have been discussed earlier in this textbook. These include the borrowing resolution if the borrower is a corporation, and if the borrower is a partnership, the agreement under which the partners operate may be required. Business and personal financial statements normally are required. These should be signed by the appropriate individuals unless they have been audited and carry an auditor's opinion.

NOTE

The note is the borrower's written promise to repay, at the agreed upon date, the loan proceeds plus interest for the time the funds are used. The note states how and when the loan will be repaid: in a lump sum on a specific date, in installments or on demand. If the loan is secured, the note will include a description of the collateral and set forth the lender's rights pertaining to the collateral. The note must include the date, the name and address of the lender and must be signed by the borrower as well as the cosigners or guarantors, if any.

The exact form of the note will vary from one lending situation to another. Normally a different form of note is used for an unsecured loan than a secured loan. Also, the exact wording of notes varies from state to state and perhaps from lender to lender within a given state.

SECURITY AGREEMENT

The purpose of the security agreement is to establish the lender's rights in the specified collateral (see Chapter 3). These rights are referred to as the security interest.

The security agreement may be a separate form or it may be combined with the note. It may be a general security agreement or it may be specialized; for example, a security agreement covering accounts receivable. Whatever its form, it will include a description of the collateral it covers.

Security Interest–Attached

Under the Uniform Commercial Code a *security interest* is any interest in personal property that results from the pledge of that property to secure a loan. The term personal property is very broad, encompassing almost everything that is not real property.

When the security interest is attached, the lender has simply established its security interest. For collateral held by the lender, such as stocks or bonds, the security interest attaches as a result of possession. For most other forms of collateral, the security interest attaches when the security agreement is completed and signed. However, the attached security interest does not assure the lender that it will have access to the collateral if the borrower fails to repay the loan. For example, the borrower might sell the collateral sometime after receiving the loan proceeds. The buyer, who paid cash for the collateral and has possession, is not likely to be willing to turn the collateral over to the lender. The buyer could claim no knowledge that the assets had been pledged.

Obviously, a lender must be able to protect its security interest from claims of other parties that may arise after the lender's security interest is attached. The UCC provides for perfection of security interests, a process that is intended to give public notice of the collateral position taken by the lender.

FINANCING STATEMENT

For collateral remaining in the possession of the borrower, perfection of the security interest usually requires completion and filing of a financing statement. The form used for the financing statement derives from the Uniform Commercial Code and usually carries the designation UCC-1. The form varies somewhat from state to state, and each version must be approved by that state's secretary of state. The completed form lists the names and addresses of the borrower and lender as well as a description of the collateral. The form must be signed by both the borrower (debtor) and the lender (secured party).

Security Interest–Perfected

The completed financing statement must be filed with the appropriate public official in order for the security interest to be perfected. Normally, the public official is the secretary of state or the county clerk, depending on the classification of the borrower. Once the filing is complete, the lender's interest in the collateral has legal precedence over any interests that may come about later.

Filing a financing statement is not the only method of perfecting a security interest. In some states, the security interest in an asset that carries a title (vehicles or aircraft) is perfected by showing the lien position on the title through the state's registration process.

Possession may be sufficient to perfect the security interest for collateral that the lender can hold, such as stock or bond certificates. Obviously, collateral cannot be sold if the lender has possession of it. However, many assets may also require some form of assignment in order for the lender to feel its rights are secure. Loans against the cash value of life insurance policies normally require an assignment that is sent to the insurance company. Acknowledgement from the insurance company then assures the lender its collateral position is protected.

LOAN AGREEMENT

The loan agreement is the contract between the borrower and the lender. The common features of term loan agreements were described in Chapter 4. Many lenders do not require loan agreements on the simpler forms of loans. However, even in simple lending arrangements, a loan agreement can be valuable to the lender. The agreement provides protective measures for the lender that otherwise might not be established (see Chapter 4).

STOCK AND BOND POWERS

Some commercial loans are secured by stocks and bonds. These securities normally are held by the lender. In case of default, the lender must be able to sell the securities. The lender could have the borrower sign the securities, thus making them transferable. This is not a good policy because after a loan is paid off, the borrower would once again take possession of the securities. With the signatures affixed, the securities would be much the same as negotiable instruments. To avoid this problem, lenders use a limited power of attorney called a stock (or bond) power. This is signed by the borrower and held by the lender. If the borrower defaults and sale of the securities is required, the signed *stock (or bond) power* serves the same function as signed certificates. When the loan is paid off, the stock power is destroyed.

OTHER DOCUMENTATION

Many other documents may be required or desirable in specific lending situations. Documentation is a legalistic subject, so the views of one lender as to the appropriate documents and their make-up may differ from the views of another lender in the same area. A person working in commercial lending should devote a significant amount of time to studying the documentation requirements of the organization. Proper documentation can mean the difference between success and failure in a commercial lending situation.

LOAN FOLLOW-UP

The loan officer who handled the loan application may be responsible for the follow-up. In a large organization, follow-up might be assigned to another officer specializing in that function. That person may be referred to as the account officer. Among the many follow-up duties, one of the most important is maintaining communication with the borrower.

COMMUNICATION WITH THE BORROWER

There are two major reasons for maintaining communication with the borrower after the loan is made. The first is that if the borrowing firm is successful in its future operations, the lender will want the future borrowing and deposit business of the firm. And, if the borrower is prosperous, any number of competitors will attempt to secure the firm's deposits and attempt to meet its borrowing needs. Maintaining good communication with the borrower will help prevent the success of competitors.

The second reason is that the lender wants to know as much as possible, as soon as possible, about developments that might interfere with repayment of the loan. Presumably a positive relationship existed between the borrower and lender at the time the loan was made. If this good relationship can be maintained, the chances are good that the borrower will keep deposits and loans with the lender. It is also more likely that the lender will be informed of any developing problems or major changes that could affect the loan.

Obvious concerns of the account officer in observing the borrower's firm include declining sales, lawsuits and loss of major customers. However, other developments could suggest emerging problems. These might include unexpected management changes, labor problems or developing competition. The account officer should always be concerned with a firm's decision to undertake a major expansion. Such a step could absorb much of a firm's liquidity and impair its debt repayment ability. The sooner the lender knows of developing changes in a firm, the sooner it can consider taking defensive steps.

OTHER FOLLOW-UP MEASURES

Very few commercial loans are weak loans at the time they are made. However, the deterioration that will eventually make a loan weak can appear at any time. It may be due to declining economic conditions, increased competition, changes within the firm or a combination of reasons. The account officer should follow procedures designed to help detect problems within borrowing firms. Those discussed below are among the most important.

Continued Analysis of Financial Statements

Perhaps the most important follow-up measure is to perform periodic financial statement analysis. Since a tremendous amount of deterioration can take place in a short time, it is preferable to receive statements from firms on a quarterly basis. These statements should be analyzed and the results placed on a spread sheet as described in Chapter 5. This analysis will point out any negative trends that may be developing.

The reason for any significant change in the financial statements should be determined. For example, if accounts payable declined sharply from one balance sheet to the next, but the latter balance sheet showed a large notes payable, which was not on earlier statements, it could be assumed that the firm is having trouble paying its trade debt on time. Suppliers may have required notes payable to strengthen their creditor positions. Increasing pressure from the suppliers to collect the notes may impair the firm's ability to meet its obligation to the lender.

Monitoring Compliance with Loan Agreements

The account officer should verify from time to time that the borrower is not violating any requirements of the loan agreement. Breach of any covenants will constitute default. For example, the agreement may include a requirement that working capital be maintained at or above a certain level. The purpose of this covenant is to assure that the firm's liquidity remains sufficiently high so that its ability to make payments on the loan is not impaired.

If it is determined from the borrower's latest financial statements that the working capital requirement is being violated, immediate steps should be taken. The most extreme step would be to call the loan as the agreement allows given an act of default by the borrower. If it is determined that this step is appropriate, the value of the loan agreement is obvious. The agreement allows the lender to call the loan much sooner than would have been possible if it had been necessary to wait until payments were in default.

Hopefully, it will not be necessary to call the loan. The borrower may be suffering only a temporary liquidity decline, and, after discussions with the borrower, the lender may grant a temporary waiver of the covenant. Another possible step would be to revise the covenant in favor of the borrower. This should be done only if it is decided the covenant is too restrictive.

Periodic Review of Loan Documentation

The documents supporting a loan should be checked periodically to make sure that they are in order, particularly those pertaining to collateral. For example, a filing statement is effective for five years if there was no maturity date specified at the time of the original filing. If a maturity date was specified, the filing is good to that maturity date plus sixty days, up to a limit of five years. If the original loan spanned more than five years, or if loans have been renewed without filing new financial statements, the period of the filing may elapse and perfection of the security interest will be lost.

Other items that should be checked along with documentation include evidence of insurance coverage and accounts receivable aging schedules. One of the first expenses to be cut by many financially troubled firms is insurance premiums. If an important coverage lapses, it is possible that the lender's collateral interest is in jeopardy and that the firm may be in financial difficulty.

The aging schedule should be checked for significant increases in past due accounts. This can be important even if the receivables are not the security for the loan because of the indication it provides of future problems for the borrower.

Checking Account Balances

The balances in a borrower's checking account may be a lead indicator of problems. A low or overdrawn checking account could indicate liquidity problems within the firm. Unusually low balances or overdrafts may prompt the account officer to check with other institutions where the borrower maintains accounts or has loans. It may be desirable to conduct a credit investigation much as was done prior to the loan's approval.

Collateral Control

A vital part of loan follow-up is collateral control. The control procedures to be followed depend on the nature of the collateral. Control of floored inventories by means of flooring inspections was discussed in Chapter 3. Chapter 6 included control considerations when accounts receivable serve as collateral. As a general concept, collateral control means: 1) making sure that the lender does not lose access to the collateral in case it becomes necessary to take possession and 2) doing as much as possible to prevent a decline in the value of the collateral.

For some loans collateral control may seem deceptively easy. For example, a loan to the owner of a business operated as a proprietorship might be secured by 1,000 shares of the common stock of a major corporation. Perhaps the stock has been in the businessperson's family for years and he or she does not want to sell it.

The stock is traded on the New York Stock Exchange, so the lender has no trouble determining its value. It can be assumed the lender advances 60 percent of the market value of the shares. The lender holds the stock certificates along with signed stock powers so sale can be effected if necessary.

The collateral is controlled in the sense that the lender has it locked away. However, the lender has no control over the value of the collateral. The stock's market value could decline sharply, say by

60 or 65 percent. If the market value of the stock is not monitored, and sale becomes necessary because the borrower defaults, the lender could be surprised to find the stock's value is well below the loan balance.

If the shares of stock pledged by the businessperson split three for one, the corporation would send the stockholder 2,000 additional shares. The lender would not receive the shares because the businessperson is on the books of the corporation as owner of the original 1,000 shares. Since the corporation would then have three times as many shares outstanding, the market value of each share after the split would be approximately one-third as much as it would have been had there been no split. Thus, the lender is suddenly in the position of having only one-third as much collateral as it intended to have.

This example suggests that collateral control cannot be treated casually. Whether control procedures consist of periodic checks of equipment to make sure it is in place and well maintained, flooring inspections, audits of accounts receivable or other measures, they must be considered a vital part of loan administration.

LOAN REVIEW

Many lenders may not have a separate loan review function. If not, the steps discussed here should be combined with loan follow-up measures in some manner. It is preferable to have a distinct loan review function conducted by individuals other than those who process the loan applications, perform the credit analysis and conduct the loan follow-up activities. In this way, loan review is an audit function that not only monitors the commercial loan portfolio but also measures the performance of those who made the commercial loans. This approach becomes more necessary once the commercial lending function becomes so large that senior management cannot adequately oversee all aspects of the activity.

PURPOSES OF LOAN REVIEW

Viewed as a separate function, commercial loan review has two broad purposes:

1. Assure compliance with commercial loan policy;
2. Identify problem loans as soon as possible.

The elements of a commercial loan policy were discussed in Chapter 6. Not only should policy set forth such requirements as the method of loan pricing, maturity guidelines and acceptable collateral but also such concerns as the types of loans to be emphasized and a quality standard for these loans. The loan review process should keep senior management informed as to how well these policy requirements are being met. Additionally, if policy is inappropriate or unworkable in certain aspects, loan review should identify these problems.

IDENTIFYING PROBLEM LOANS

Ideally, loan review would detect problems before they became so serious that the repayment of the loan was threatened. This is an overly optimistic view because some problems defy early detection, but a comprehensive loan review process will provide some "early warning" signals.

Some of the follow-up procedures discussed earlier might be considered part of loan review. For example, it probably does not matter who conducts the periodic review of documents as long as it is done. In addition, the account officer should be just as concerned about looking for early warning signs as the person conducting the loan review. Some of the early signs of possible problems are listed in Figure 10-1.

Figure 10-1. Early Indicators of Possible Loan Problems

- Late financial statements
- Change of auditors
- Qualified audit opinion
- Refusal to provide audited statements
- Calling officer unable to get appointment
- Notice of legal action against borrower
- Resignation or firing of management personnel
- Loss of trade credit—cash only
- Frequent "crash" sales
- Loss of major customers
- Loss of major product line or franchise
- Notice of cancelled insurance
- Major change in lifestyle of owner/manager
- Undertaking a new, high-risk venture
- No planned management succession
- Poor organization
- Poor maintenance practices

The items in Figure 10-1 could no doubt be expanded. Also, the list does not include items of information produced by financial statement analysis (see Chapter 5), receivables aging schedules and other information sources discussed earlier. Of course, by the time a problem reveals itself in the financial statements, it is already well advanced. Indicators such as those listed above may give warning signals much sooner.

CORRECTIVE ACTIONS

Along with its major purpose of early detection of problems, loan review should suggest corrective actions. It should be noted, however, that there is a danger of moving too soon. A lender should not react too quickly to a warning signal when, in fact, the business is not in any difficulty. If early warning signals suggest problems, these should be confirmed before the borrower is approached to discuss a solution. This confirmation may be accomplished by a visit which is within the usual pattern of visits to the firm or by checking other sources.

As soon as it is evident that the borrower has a developing problem, the lender should arrange a meeting to discuss corrective actions. One or more of the steps discussed here may be appropriate if the problem has not reached a point where the lender feels it must call the loan.

Additions of Capital

The lender may be able to convince the owners to add more capital to the firm. A proprietor who may have all of his or her capital committed to the business may be able to find a partner who would be able to add capital. A corporation may be able to sell additional shares of stock.

Curtailing Expansion Plans

In order to alleviate a developing problem, the borrower may need to scale back or eliminate projects which, if carried on, will absorb the firm's working capital. Such plans may be pet projects which, though desired by the borrower, may not be economically feasible.

Forcing Collection of Slow Receivables

In difficult economic periods, many of the borrower's credit customers may become slow payers. The lender may be able to assist in, or at least encourage, speeding up the collection process.

Improving Inventory Management

The borrower may have excessive inventories of slow-moving items. It might be preferable to sell such items at sizable discounts, even though such sales might result in losses, in order to generate enough funds to avoid defaulting on loan payments.

Counselling the Borrower

The lender should plan for its officers to spend a significant amount of time and effort advising the problem borrower. The lender may want to bring in outside experts to counsel the firm. It must be remembered that it is in everyone's best interests to keep the firm alive and operating.

Obtaining Additional Collateral

Requiring additional collateral from a borrower is an indirect help for the borrower. This is because if the lender can improve its protection, it may feel less need to call the loan when default occurs. Obtaining additional collateral may also enable the lender to justify restructuring the loan to reduce pressure on the borrower.

Obtaining Guarantees

The guarantee of a third party may be obtainable even though a firm is beginning to develop problems. For example, the guarantor may be a major stockholder, an affiliated company or a major supplier who does not want to lose an important outlet for its product. A guarantee also may allow debt restructuring.

Debt Restructuring

If a firm has a promising future but is having short-term problems, the lender may consider lengthening the loan terms, allow interest-only payments for a period of time or in some other manner rewrite the original loan in order to reduce financial pressure on the borrower. It may be that the borrower's need is for a long-term loan that is justified by cash flow projections. The borrower may replace part of a short-term obligation with a longer-term loan. The firm may even bring in another lending institution to make the loan if the firm's future appears solid.

Increase the Loan

An increase in the loan is seldom an attractive corrective measure. It should be allowed only if the firm makes major changes that clearly remove the cause of the problem. However, even though lending more money rarely can be justified, it frequently is a temptation to loan officers to do so when a firm begins to show signs of trouble. The borrower is convinced that the problem can be resolved if only more money is made available. The loan officer may fear that denying additional funds will cause the firm to fail and that some additional funds will enable the firm to pull out of its problems. Usually the result is greater exposure and bigger problems for the lender.

PROBLEM LOANS

Just when a lender might choose to designate a loan as a problem loan depends on the views of the individual. To many, a loan would become a problem as soon as any signs of difficulty appeared. Here a problem loan is considered one which cannot be repaid as originally intended. In other words, the lender must look to secondary sources of repayment.

CALLING THE LOAN

If the borrower has committed one or more acts of default and the lender determines that any corrective actions almost certainly would fail, little alternative remains except to call the loan. The lender's legal counsel should be involved in the decision and should assist in preparing a letter to the borrower demanding immediate and full payment.

Normally lenders who hold deposits can employ what is termed right of offset if it holds deposits of the defaulted borrower. This allows the lender to apply any deposits of the borrower toward payment of the debt.

Calling a loan probably will not produce full payment. Default by the borrower usually includes a failure to make payments due to lack of funds. If the borrower could not make payment on the loan there is little reason to believe full payment is possible when the loan is called. However, the loan must be called before the lender can institute actions to foreclose on collateral and/or sue the borrower for payment.

AVOIDING THE COURTS

Out-of-court settlement of the debt may be possible. This process becomes less feasible and more cumbersome the greater the number of creditors and the more extreme the financial problems of the borrower. The advantages of an out-of-court settlement should be lower expenses and a more rapid settlement. An out-of-court settlement not only requires cooperation of creditors with one another but also cooperation of the borrower with the creditors. The firm must work with the lenders in working out the sale of assets. However, many borrowers will resist the takeover and sale of assets by creditors. When legal foreclosure is likely, the creditor may choose bankruptcy.

BANKRUPTCY

Bankruptcy is a legal process and is governed by the Bankruptcy Reform Act of 1978. The Act became effective October 1, 1979. Bankruptcy may be initiated voluntarily by a financially distressed firm or by creditors of the firm. Creditors may initiate bankruptcy proceedings if they feel the borrower is dissipating the assets of the firm.

REORGANIZATION UNDER BANKRUPTCY

Bankruptcy does not necessarily mean a firm will go out of business. If filing is under Chapter 11 of the Act, reorganization of the debtor is attempted with court supervision. The court protects the debtor firm from its creditors while reorganization ensues. A reorganization plan must be submitted outlining the steps the firm will take. The court and a sufficient number of the firm's creditors must accept the plan. The plan may, for example, allow the firm to eliminate its debts through partial and/or delayed payments and replace some secured debt with unsecured notes.

Small proprietorships are treated under Chapter 13 of the Act if unsecured claims are less than $100,000 and secured claims are less than $350,000. Chapter 13 allows payment to be made over a 36-month period, if possible. If it does not appear possible for the firm to eliminate its debts in 36 months, the firm may be required to proceed under Chapter 11. Chapter 13 is preferable because it is simpler and less expensive.

If a debtor firm is able to negotiate a reorganization plan with its creditors, it may be able to retire its debts and emerge from bankruptcy as a viable and productive company. If a reorganization plan cannot be reached, liquidation is the only alternative.

LIQUIDATION UNDER BANKRUPTCY

Liquidation of a debtor firm is governed by Chapter 7 of the Bankruptcy Reform Act. This recourse is taken when the court believes the firm cannot be salvaged in viable form. Many creditors may prefer liquidation if they believe that the process will produce better repayment results.

If liquidation is required, the federal bankruptcy court appoints a referee who then meets with the creditors. At the meeting, claims are proved and a trustee is elected by the creditors. The trustee is charged with the responsibility of seeing to the orderly liquidation of the debtor's assets and distribution of the proceeds to the creditors. This is usually an expensive and prolonged process.

PREVENTIVE MEASURES

A few loans will always become problem loans. Changing economic conditions, increased competition and other developments will create unexpected problems for some borrowers. If a lender never experiences a problem loan, it will be guilty of turning away a great many deserving borrowers. However, the lender must try to prevent problem loans from becoming more than a very small percentage of the loan portfolio. The best preventive measures are careful execution of the steps leading to the lending decision and proper administration of the loans that are made.

SUMMARY

Commercial loan administration includes those functions that should be performed once the decision to grant a loan is made. Appropriate documentation must be assembled. In the case of secured commercial loans, much of the required documentation derives from the Uniform Commercial Code.

The responsibility for loan follow-up must be assigned. Follow-up procedures include maintaining customer communication, analysis of financial statements when received, monitoring compliance with loan agreements, periodic review of loan documentation, monitoring the borrower's deposit accounts and collateral control procedures.

Loan review may or may not be a function distinct from loan follow-up. As a distinct function it would have two major purposes: to assure compliance with loan policy and to identify developing loan problems.

If developing loan problems are detected, the lender may be able to apply one or more corrective measures to help eliminate the problem.

If the loan deteriorates to the point at which the lender must look to a secondary source of repayment, it may be necessary to call the loan.

The lender may be able to work in a cooperative manner with the borrower to sell assets and otherwise try to generate funds to repay the loan. If not, bankruptcy may be the only alternative. Bankruptcy proceedings will be oriented toward either reorganization of the firm, or if there is no chance of its survival as a viable company, liquidation of its assets and distribution of the proceeds to creditors.

CHAPTER QUESTIONS

1. What information should be on the note which evidences a loan?
2. What is a security agreement? A financing statement?
3. What is a security interest? How is it perfected?
4. What are four important steps in loan follow-up procedures?
5. What is the purpose of collateral control?
6. Viewed as an activity conducted outside the credit or loan department, what are the two main objectives of loan review?
7. What are four corrective actions which might be taken as soon as a loan appears to be developing problems?
8. Define bankruptcy. Distinguish between reorganization and liquidation under bankruptcy.

Glossary

Accelerated depreciation: Methods of computing depreciation whereby the depreciation charges are higher in the first years of an asset's life than in succeeding years.

Accounts payable: Short-term obligations owed by a firm to its suppliers of goods and services.

Accounts receivable: Short-term obligations owed to a firm by customers for goods or services sold to them.

Acid test ratio: A more stringent test of a firm's liquidity than the current ratio, computed by dividing current assets less inventory by current liabilities.

Adverse opinion: An auditor's statement indicating major exceptions have been found in the reporting processes.

Aging schedule: A schedule showing the age of the accounts receivable owned by a firm as of a given date.

Amortize: The payment of the principal amount of a loan in stages over a period of time.

Assets: The items owned by an individual or business, including property rights.

Balance sheet: The financial statement that sets forth the assets, liabilities and net worth (owner's equity) of an individual or business as of a certain date.

Balloon payment: The final payment on a loan that is much larger than preceding payments, perhaps totalling 40 or 50 percent of the loan principal.

Bankruptcy: The legal status of a firm (or person) which is unable to pay its debts when its assets are placed under administration of the court.

Bond: Evidence of a debt; the issuer of the bond is usually obligated to pay the bondholder a fixed sum at a stated future date and to pay interest at a specified rate to that date. Bonds may be issued by corporations, the federal government, and state and local governments.

Book value: The amount at which an asset is carried on a company's balance sheet. Also the amount of owner's equity for a company.

Breakeven analysis: Determining the level of sales or production at which total costs and total revenue are equal.

Budget: A projection of a facet of a firm's activity for a future period, such as a cash budget.

Business cycle: A period that includes a general decline and a subsequent general advance in economic activity.

Capital: The long-term investment in a business consisting of long-term debt, paid-in equity and retained earnings.

Capital market: Financial markets for long-term debt obligations and equity securities.

Cash budget: A projection of a firm's cash inflows, outflows and balances for a certain period.

Cash cycle: The process by which cash follows a route through inventory, accounts receivable and back to cash.

Cash flow: The net cash resulting from a firm's operations during a reporting period; usually measured as net income plus noncash expenses.

Collateral: Something of value pledged by or on behalf of a borrower to secure a loan; in case of default, the lender's claim to the collateral is exercised to satisfy the debt.

Commercial paper: Short-term, unsecured corporate debt evidenced by a negotiable promise to pay, issued by a company wishing to borrow money for a short period (up to 270 days) and generally bought by another corporation.

Compensating balance: Deposits required from a borrowing company by a financial institution as a condition for obtaining the loan.

Compound interest: Interest that is earned on interest accumulated in earlier periods.

Corporation: A business form requiring a charter, normally from a state, the owners of which are not personally liable for the firm's debts.

Covenant: A constraint in a loan agreement that sets forth certain requirements as to what the borrower will and will not do.

Credit file: A central information source compiled for use by the lender. As a minimum, contents of the file include interview notes, correspondence, copies of financial statements and a record of other loans made to the applicant. Signed notes, titles and warehouse receipts are not maintained in this file.

Credit risk: That element of making a loan that is an indication of the chance that the loan will be repaid. It is determined through the credit analysis process, including a judgment factor.

Current assets: A firm's assets consisting of cash or items which can be expected to convert to cash in one year or less.

Current ratio: A basic indicator of a firm's liquidity, computed by dividing current assets by current liabilities.

Demand deposit: Deposits held at depository institutions that the owner can withdraw by check.

Depreciation: Deducting part of the cost of an asset from income in each year of the asset's life.

Depression: An extended period of severe decline in business activity, employment and profits.

Disclaimer opinion: An auditor's statement indicating that the audit was so limited (or nonexistent) that no conclusions can be reached by the auditor.

Discount: May refer to deduction of interest from the face amount of a note when a loan is made, or to trade discounts given to firms for payment of invoices within a specified early period.

Discount rate: The interest rate charged on loans to financial institutions that borrow from the Federal Reserve System.

Diversification: The process of acquiring a portfolio of assets with different risk-return characteristics in order to reduce overall risk.

Dun & Bradstreet: A firm that provides credit information about other companies.

Earnings: A company's income after all expenses including noncash expenses.

Equity: The ownership value of a business.

Factoring: A financing method where the firm sells its accounts receivable to a financial institution.

Federal funds: Financial institution deposits held at Federal Reserve Banks. These balances may be loaned (borrowed) through the Federal funds market.

Federal Home Loan Bank System: The central credit facility for all federally chartered savings and loan associations, mutual savings banks, and member state-chartered savings associations and life insurance companies.

Federal Reserve System: The central banking system of the United States. Its major responsibility is the conduct of monetary policy.

Financial intermediary: A financial institution that accepts money from savers and investors, and uses those funds to make loans and other investments in its own name; includes savings associations, mutual savings banks, life insurance companies, credit unions and investment companies.

Financial leverage: The use of borrowed funds in an effort to increase the return on equity.

First-in, first-out (FIFO): A method of valuing inventories and determining cost of goods sold that assumes the first items of inventory purchased were those sold.

Fiscal policy: The federal government's taxing and budgeting process.

Fixed assets: Land, buildings and equipment which are used by the firm in the normal course of business and not held for sale.

Fixed costs: The costs of a firm which remain constant regardless of the level of production.

Floor planning: Loans to dealers to finance large ticket inventory items.

Funded debt: A firm's long-term debt.

Goodwill: An intangible asset of a firm, usually the result of buying another firm for more than book value.

Guarantor: The individual or entity that guarantees to repay a debt if the borrower defaults.

High credit: The highest level of credit owed by a firm during a specified period.

Holding company: A company that holds enough voting stock in one or more other companies to have control.

Income Statement: The financial statement that measures the income over expenses of a firm over a period of time.

Inflation: A persistent rise in the average level of prices.

Interest rate risk: The risk embodied in an asset that its value will decline as a result of rising interest rates.

Investment tax credit: An income tax credit given to firms that purchase plant and equipment.

Joint venture: A project, usually of a limited duration, undertaken by two or more companies.

Junior debt: Debt that has a subordinated claim to the firm's earnings or assets.

Key-person insurance: A life insurance policy on one of the key individuals in a business, payable to the business.

Last-in, first-out (LIFO): A method of valuing inventories and determining cost of goods sold that assumes the most recent inventory purchased was that sold.

Lease: A contractual arrangement between the owner (lessor) of an asset and the user (lessee) of the asset which requires the lessee to pay the lessor certain payments during the lease period.

Letter of credit: An agreement by a financial institution that it will advance funds if certain conditions are met.

Leverage: See financial leverage and operating leverage.

Liability: Any debt or obligation of a company or individual.

Lien: A legal claim against property owned by another, usually resulting from pledge of the property as collateral.

Limited partnership: A partnership consisting of one or more limited partners whose liability is limited to their investments, and one or more general partners who are responsible for all partnership debts.

Line of credit: Advance approval by a commercial lender to provide a firm credit up to a specified level for a specified period.

Liquidation: Sale of all of a firm's assets when the company is dissolved, usually as a result of bankruptcy.

Liquidity: The quality of an asset that refers to the amount of time required and risk of loss encountered in its conversion to cash; also the ability of a firm to meet its current obligations.

Matching principle: The view that a business entity should finance short-term assets with short-term liabilities and long-term assets with long-term liabilities and equity.

Money market: Financial markets in which short-term debt instruments such as commercial paper and Treasury bills are traded.

Monetary policy: Policy of the Federal Reserve designed to control the money supply in order to influence economic activity.

Money supply: Money is defined in various ways but the most used definition, called M1, consists of currency, coin, demand deposits, NOW accounts and traveler's checks held by the public.

NOW account: A savings deposit transferable to a third party by use of a negotiable order of withdrawal.

Note: A written promise to pay a stipulated sum of money to a specified party under conditions mutually agreed upon.

Open-market operations: Buying and selling of government securities by the Federal Reserve in its conduct of monetary policy.

Operating leverage: The degree to which fixed costs comprise a firm's total costs. *See* breakeven analysis.

Partnership: A firm owned by two or more persons each of whom is personally liable for the firm's debts.

Permanent current assets: A term used to describe the minimum level of current assets required for normal operation.

Primary markets: The markets in which securities are originally issued.

Prime rate: The interest rate that commercial banks charge their most creditworthy borrowers.

Principal: The capital sum of a loan, as distinguished from interest or charges.

Pro forma statements: Projected financial statements for some specified future period.

Proprietorship: A form of business organization with a single owner who bears unlimited liability, owns the assets and is entitled to the profits of the firm.

Qualified opinion: An auditor's statement issued when the auditor has some questions or uncertainty regarding one or more reporting methods.

Quick ratio: See acid test ratio.

Recession: The phase of the business cycle during which economic activity, profits and employment decline.

Required reserves: Financial institutions are required by law to hold minimum reserves equal to a percent of their deposits and certain other liabilities. Reserves are held in vault cash or at the Federal Reserve Bank.

Retained earnings: The net worth account which represents past earnings which have been reinvested in the business.

Return on equity ratio: The most important of all financial ratios computed, it measures the rate of return on funds invested in a company.

Revolving credit agreement: A commitment under which funds can be borrowed, repaid and reborrowed during the period of the agreement.

Risk: The probability that future returns will be less than expected returns.

Rule of 72: The rule of thumb based on the mathematical fact that dividing 72 by the interest rate earned on an investment will give the (approximate) number of years required for compounding to double the original investment.

Rule of 78s: Method of recognizing add-on interest by using predetermined factors to determine the portion of total interest earned for the period.

Secondary market: The market activity of securities after original issue.

Secured loan: A loan backed by pledged collateral.

Security: An investment instrument such as a stock or bond.

Security agreement: That section of the note or a separate document describing the loan collateral. It establishes the lender's rights in the specified collateral.

Security interest: Interest in collateral that secures payment or performance of an obligation.

Small Business Administration: A federal agency established to provide various forms of assistance to small businesses.

Source: A decrease in an asset, increase in a liability or increase in owner's equity.

Sources and uses of funds statement: The financial statement which shows the cash flows between balance sheet accounts during a reporting period.

Straight line depreciation: Depreciation charged at a level rate over the depreciable life of an asset.

Term loan: A loan with a maturity greater than one year with repayment in installments.

Trade credit: Credit provided by suppliers as a result of purchase of their products.

Treasury bills: Obligations of the federal government with initial maturities of three, six or twelve months.

Trend analysis: Analysis of a firm's performance made over several periods in order to detect significant patterns.

Trust receipt: An instrument acknowledging that the borrower holds items of inventory for sale in trust for the lender.

Uniform Commercial Code: A body of business-related laws dealing with sale of goods, their transportation and delivery, financing, storage and final payment.

Unqualified opinion: An auditor's statement describing the scope of the audit, essentially stating that the financial statement "presents fairly" the financial position of the company.

Unsecured loan: A loan which includes no specific pledge of assets.

Use: An increase in assets, decrease in liability or decrease in owner's equity.

Variable costs: The portion of a firm's costs which vary directly with production.

Warehouse receipt: A receipt issued by a warehouse company acknowledging storage of specified goods.

Working capital: The portion of a firm's long-term debt and equity which finances current assets; current assets minus current liabilities.

Yield: The rate of return on an investment, normally expressed as an annual rate.

Yield curve: A graph showing the relationship between the yields and maturities of a certain class of securities, e.g., U.S. government securities.

Appendix

Code of Ethics for the Exchange of Commercial Credit Information Between Banks

FOREWORD

The basic precepts of RMA's Code of Ethics have existed since 1916 and remain virtually unchanged. In 1976, RMA appointed a select committee to evaluate the Code of Ethics and its use in the current banking environment. This committee revised the Code by reducing the number of Articles, developing comments to explain each Article and simplifying the language used. The group also approved a revised symbol (logo) for use by banks on their stationery to show they are RMA members and Code subscribers. Both the revised Code and the new logo were approved by RMA's Board of Directors in June 1976.

Over 150,000 copies of the revised Code have been distributed since 1976, evidencing its wide acceptance by the banking industry.

This April 1980 reprinting contains some minor modifications. First, the Preamble and Article 3, Comment 5 have been amplified in regard to the securities laws. Second, the title now states that the Code applies to the exchange of commercial credit information between banks.

Those involved in the credit information exchange process should become familiar with two additional documents. Through the efforts of RMA and the National Association of Credit Management, a joint Statement of Principles for the Exchange of Credit Information Between Banks and Business Credit Grantors is available. RMA has also developed Guidelines for the Exchange of Foreign Credit Information.

RMA believes that one way to maintain professionalism in credit information exchange is for all banks to adhere to the Articles of the Code of Ethics which follow.

Robert Morris Associates

April 1980

PREAMBLE

Robert Morris Associates, recognizing the importance of the free and responsible exchange of information in the credit-based American economic system, originally adopted this Code of Ethics in 1916. Since then, the Code has become the ethical standard for conduct in the exchange of commercial credit information. Although intended to relate to information exchange between banks, the precepts of the Code have served as the foundation for all commercial credit information exchange.

Adherence to this Code of Ethics is essential. Upon joining RMA, members acknowledge and agree to abide by these principles, and they expect others with whom information is exchanged to respect them also.

This code is designed for commercial transactions, and its use is subject to applicable federal and state laws. Such laws include securities statutes regulating disclosure of material inside information and other laws affecting the exchange of credit information. In particular circumstances, these could include the antitrust laws, credit reporting regulations, and limitations on the use of confidential records and customer information or computerized data.

Since under the securities laws, "material inside (nonpublic) information" may, in some cases, be neither disclosed nor withheld as to transactions in connection with the sale or purchase of a security, care should be exercised and the advice of counsel sought where any such inside information may be in the possession of the respondent.

ARTICLE 1

There are two cardinal principles in the exchange of credit information: confidentiality and accuracy of inquiries and replies. This includes the identity of inquirers and sources which cannot be disclosed without their permission. Adherence to these and the other principles embodied in this Code is essential, since offenders jeopardize their privilege to participate further in the exchange of credit information.

COMMENTS

Confidentiality, as it is used here, is based on the reliance placed upon the fidelity of another with whom information is being exchanged. A trust is placed in all parties involved that the information has been requested for a legitimate purpose and will not be used indiscriminately.

When conducting investigations, the identity of the inquirer should not be divulged without its authorization. Similarly, the identity of the source of the information should not be made known without its authorization.

The facts presented must be accurate because the bank reference is one of the most pertinent sources of credit information. When discussing data, favorable or unfavorable, the responding bank must give a reply that is restricted to or based on fact. If a discrepancy is discovered within a reasonable time after an inquiry has been answered, and is considered to be significant in relation to the purpose of the inquiry, it is prudent and ethical that the discrepancy be disclosed to the inquirer.

It is expected that, as a matter of professional courtesy, no liability will be attached to or result from the good faith exchange of information.

If the information is for a customer, it should be screened according to the customer's needs, credit sophistication and ability to handle the information discreetly.

Adherence to these and the other principles embodied in this Code of Ethics is essential. Violations of the Code could damage the reputation of offending banks and individuals. If they demonstrate an inability and/or unwillingness to handle and exchange credit information responsibly, they risk losing the privilege.

In addition, violations of the Code by RMA member banks may lead to the termination of their membership in the association, in accordance with Section 2.07 of the RMA By-Laws.

ARTICLE 2

Each inquiry should specifically indicate its purpose and the amount involved.

COMMENTS

One of the most important elements of an inquiry is its purpose. The bank receiving the inquiry has a right to know why the information is needed. If no purpose is given, there is no obligation to respond. Knowing and understanding the purpose of an inquiry places the recipient in a better position to respond with the type and amount of information needed to satisfy the inquirer. When the purpose of the inquiry is solicitation, acquisition, merger, competition, or actual or contemplated legal action, reply is at the discretion of the bank of account.

The inquirer should state the initial steps taken, as well as the information on hand, in order to avoid duplication of effort.

The legitimate use of credit information is to assist an inquirer who expects to extend credit or otherwise rely on the subject of the inquiry in business dealings. An inquiry should not be answered without first determining its legitimacy and establishing the identity of the inquirer. For example, when receiving a telephone inquiry, information should not be disclosed on the first call unless the inquirer is known and identified. A return call will usually establish the identity of the inquirer.

In the majority of instances, a specific amount is involved in the transaction which generates an inquiry. When initial trade credit is involved and no amount is established, the inquiring party should be asked for the normal size of its transactions. A range of figures such as $500-$1,000 or $50,000- $60,000 is acceptable. It is unacceptable to use fictitious figures or to inflate the amount involved to induce the responding bank to provide details beyond what may be necessary to answer the inquiry suitably. If for some reason there is no amount involved, the inquirer should state this in a manner which would logically satisfy the respondent as to the overall purpose of the inquiry.

A proper inquiry should contain the following:

1. SUBJECT: The subject of the inquiry should be identified as completely as possible including full name, address and names of the principals.

2. PURPOSE: The reason for the inquiry should be given in sufficient detail to allow the recipient to make an appropriate response.

3. EXPERIENCE: If the inquirer has had experience with the subject, a summary of that experience should be provided. Doing this creates a true exchange of information and helps to eliminate duplication of effort.

4. REQUIREMENTS: The inquirer should be specific about the information required to satisfy the needs of the inquiry, such as deposit relationships, loan experience, financial information, assessment of management, etc.

5. OTHER: Any other factors relevant to the inquiry should be disclosed.

ARTICLE 3

Responses should be prompt and disclose sufficient material facts commensurate with the purpose and amount of the inquiry. Specific questions should be given careful and frank replies.

COMMENTS

Prompt and accurate replies are signs of dependability and professionalism that help the users of the information conduct business on a timely basis. Although response time to inquiries will vary depending upon the amount of information needed, the following general guidelines are considered appropriate:

TYPE	RESPONSE TIME
Wire or cable inquiry	Within 24 hours of receipt
Telephone inquiry	Within 24 hours of receipt
Written inquiry	Within 4 days of receipt
Telephone investigation	Two working days
Written investigation	Six working days

If unusual delays are expected, the inquirer should be informed.

Once the legitimacy and the requirements of the inquiry are established, it is answered by providing a summary of the bank's experience and knowledge of the subject commensurate with the amount involved and the respondent's confidence in the inquirer.

A full response may include:

1. The opening date of the relationship
2. History of the subject
   - How long established
   - Legal form of organization
   - Names of the principals as well as their background and experience
   - Line of business
3. Demand deposit relationships
   - Opening date–if different from the opening date of the relationship
   - Average collected balances, for at least the past three months, in RMA General Figure Ranges*
   Several cautions in this area:

   A.   General figure ranges are ordinarily not used in mutual revisions. Rather, industry practice is to describe balances simply as

---

*See definition of RMA General Figure Ranges.

"compensating" (or "commensurate"), "less than compensating," etc. Or, if there is no compensating balance requirement, that fact may be revealed, followed by words such as "satisfactory," "less than satisfactory," etc.

B. Do not use the term "substantial" to describe the balances in demand deposit accounts. Also avoid "satisfactory," except in the limited situation noted in (A.) above.

C. It is not recommended that compensating balance requirements be disclosed if they exist. Exchanging information about compensating balance requirements does not, in itself, constitute an antitrust violation. However, if after such an exchange there is anything approximating parallel action manifested by similarity of term, it could be claimed that the information exchanged was used illegally. This applies to the disclosure of interest rates charged on loans as well. Like compensating balances, the rates charged are arrived at by the lending bank and the borrower on particular transactions and cannot be used by others as a basis for similar arrangements.

- Number and frequency of returns
- Rating on the account—here, words like "satisfactory," "generally satisfactory," "unsatisfactory" are appropriate.

4. Summary of the borrowing relationship, if any
   - Types of loans. If a loan is secured, describe the collateral.
   - Aggregate high credit and outstanding balances in RMA General Figure Ranges.[*] These figures may be broken down further by specific loans if the situation warrants it.
   - Guarantees and endorsements, if any, should be made known.
   - Dates, length and frequency of payouts
   - Ratings—for example, "satisfactory," "unsatisfactory," etc.
   - Interest rates charged on loans should not be disclosed because of the possibility of antitrust violations. (See comments in (3C.) above regarding compensating balance requirements.)

5. Financial statement data. Where the subject is a publicly held company publishing current financial information, the release of financial statement data will normally be in compliance with the securities laws.[**] When financial statements of nonpublicly held companies

---

[*]See definition of RMA General Figure Ranges.
[**]See comments in Preamble

are submitted to the bank, with no instructions to the contrary, a general summary of the data may usually be disclosed. This disclosure should be tempered by the respondent's confidence in the inquirer and by the amount and nature of the inquiry. The summary may consist of:

- Dates of the statements and the period they cover
- Auditor's opinion
- A description of the financial condition and trends of the subject, which should include current assets, total assets, current liabilities, net worth, sales and an indication of profitability. It is the option of the responding bank to disclose this data in actual figures or in RMA General Figure Ranges.[*] Even when financial statements are submitted in confidence, a brief general description of the company's strength, size and trends may usually be disclosed.

If comments are made regarding the financial standing of the subject, they should be based on the bank's analysis of the company, pointing out to the inquirer that "our analysis shows" or using other such wording.

It remains at the discretion of the responding bank to provide the inquirer with recommendations and opinions. If a recommendation or opinion is asked for, the account officer should be consulted unless the person answering the inquiry is authorized to provide this information.

If a respondent cannot answer specific questions brought up in the inquiry, the inquirer should be told why.

ARTICLE 4

It is not permissible when soliciting an account to make an inquiry to a competitor without frankly disclosing that the subject of the inquiry is a prospect. Reply is at the discretion of the bank of account.

COMMENTS

The free exchange of information between banks depends to a large degree on the confidence that the inquiring bank will not use the credit information it receives to solicit the respondent's accounts.

---

[*]See definition of RMA General Figure Ranges.

Providing credit information is a courtesy, and, in some instances, revealing information could jeopardize the account relationship between the responding bank and the subject.

Violations of this confidence are very serious. They not only damage the inquirer's relationship with the responding bank, but also create a guarded situation that can only impede the exchange of credit information. For this reason, when solicitation is the purpose of an inquiry, this fact must be clearly stated to the bank of account, which has the option to decline information on such inquiries.

If a bank is soliciting an account of a competitor and is asked by a customer to obtain credit information on that account, the soliciting bank should explain the ethical considerations involved and suggest that the inquiring customer contact the subject's bank directly.

All parties to credit inquiries that involve solicitation must be aware of the basic confidence inherent in the exchange of information and act in a responsible manner to preserve that confidence and trust.

ARTICLE 5

A request for information based on actual or contemplated litigation shall be clearly identified as such. Reply is at the discretion of the bank of account.

COMMENTS

When the purpose of a request for information is actual or contemplated legal action, full disclosure of this fact by the inquirer is necessary. It is clearly unethical to disguise the purpose of any inquiry. This could be detrimental to the parties involved, especially when legal action is associated with an inquiry. Under those circumstances, the potential for damages is such that all parties must exercise considerable judgment before conducting an investigation or answering an inquiry of this nature.

Whenever the bank of account is placed in a conflicting position of providing information and, at the same time, protecting its customers, the amount of information, if any, will be at the discretion of the responding bank.

ARTICLE 6

All credit correspondence, including form letters, should bear the manual signature of a responsible party.

COMMENTS

Manual signatures on all credit correspondence, both inquiries and replies, are essential. Good faith responsibility for the accuracy of the information contained in the correspondence is assumed by the signer. This is the case whether the signer gathers the information or not. The title, if any, and name of the authorized signer should also be typed or printed on the correspondence. Doing this will help to address responses correctly and to identify clearly the person to contact if questions arise regarding the inquiry or reply.

ARTICLE 7

The sharing of credit information on a mutual customer should not be more frequent than annually, unless a significant change in the relationship requires an earlier revision.

COMMENTS

Credit information on mutual customers is normally reviewed annually. It should not be necessary to inquire more frequently unless interim financial data, new items, agency information or other sources point out an actual or potential problem. Information should not be requested when there is no real need.

The bank requesting the information should give a summary of its experience first. This sharing of information by both inquirer and respondent is stressed because it prevents duplication of effort and is consistent with the cooperative spirit inherent in the exchange of credit information. On mutual revisions in particular, care should be taken regarding discussion of interest rates charged and compensating balance requirements since revealing these data could have antitrust implications.

ARTICLE 8

When multiple inquiries are made simultaneously on the same subject, the inquirer should clearly state that information from the bank's own files is sufficient.

COMMENTS

There are basically two situations under which simultaneous inquiries are made to banks within the same city: where it is known that the subject has account relationships with more than one of them, or where the subject's bank(s) of account is not known (which gives rise to what is commonly known as a "fishing expedition").

In the first instance–more than one known bank of account–courtesy dictates that each responding bank be told that research beyond its own files will not be necessary.

The second situation–"fishing"–should be avoided whenever possible. The inquiring bank should make every effort to determine the subject's bank(s) of account before initiating any inquiry.

But if for some reason the name of the bank(s) of account cannot be determined, the inquiring bank then has two courses of action open to it. It could make multiple inquiries as described above, again indicating to each bank that research beyond its own records will not be necessary. Or, preferably, it can approach just one bank in the city in question and ask if it would either conduct the investigation or at least locate the name of the bank of account–which the inquiring bank, in turn, can then approach separately. All banks, particularly RMA member banks, are encouraged to assist one another in situations like this, as long as this courtesy is not abused.

RMA GENERAL FIGURE RANGES

To ensure accuracy and consistency when exchanging credit information, the RMA General Figure Ranges should be used. It may be necessary, at times, to clarify these terms so that the inquirer and respondent are "speaking the same language."

Low 4 figures = $1,000 to $1,999
Moderate 4 figures = $2,000 to $3,999
Medium 4 figures = $4,000 to $6,999
High 4 figures = $7,000 to $9,999

The ranges are adjustable to accommodate all amounts in the following manner:

"Nominal" = under $100
"3 figures" = from $100 to $999

"4 figures" = from $1,000 to $9,999
"5 figures" = from $10,000 to $99,999
"6 figures" = from $100,000 to $999,999
and so on.

CODE OF ETHICS

ARTICLES

1. There are two cardinal principles in the exchange of credit information: confidentiality and accuracy of inquiries and replies. This includes the identity of inquirers and sources which cannot be disclosed without their permission. Adherence to these and the other principles embodied in this Code is essential, since offenders jeopardize their privilege to participate further in the exchange of credit information.

2. Each inquiry should specifically indicate its purpose and the amount involved.

3. Responses should be prompt and disclose sufficient material facts commensurate with the purpose and amount of the inquiry. Specific questions should be given careful and frank replies.

4. It is not permissible when soliciting an account to make an inquiry to a competitor without frankly disclosing that the subject of the inquiry is a prospect. Reply is at the discretion of the bank of account.

5. A request for information based on actual or contemplated litigation shall be clearly identified as such. Reply is at the discretion of the bank of account.

6. All credit correspondence, including form letters, should bear the manual signature of a responsible party.

7. The sharing of credit information on a mutual customer should not be more frequent than annually, unless a significant change in the relationship requires an earlier revision.

8. When multiple inquiries are made simultaneously on the same subject, the inquirer should clearly state that information from the bank's own files is sufficient.

Additional copies. When RMA published this revised Code of Ethics in October 1976, it mailed a complimentary copy to every individual member of the association as well as to the chief executive officer of every commercial bank in the United States.

Up to 50 copies are available free of charge; thereafter: $10 per 100 copies, plus postage. Order from the RMA National Office, 1616 Philadelphia National Bank Building, Philadelphia, PA 19107.

Index

C